**ENDORSEMENT BY....**

# Dexter R. Yager, Sr.
# Businessman/Entrepreneur

Randal Ross has not only preached in some of the world's fastest-growing churches, he also pastors one — Trinity Church in Lubbock, Texas. He has a daily radio program and is a popular conference and seminar leader.

Here's the bottom line: Randal touches thousands of lives through his ministry. More importantly, he knows what works and what doesn't work in people's lives. So, when he says that relationship-building is America's number one need, I think we should listen. More to the point, we should read his fresh, candid book, *Seven Habits of Winning Relationships*. It is written in a personal, friend-to-friend style that I like. Best of all, the pages reveal a proven pattern for fulfillment and long-term success.

For example, Randal writes about the deep need for relationships. He shares, "There are only a few principles in God's Word that govern relationships. These principles apply to *all* relationships."

Personally, I've tried to develop these relationships — even back when I worked at Sears and sold cars in Rome, New York. I have certainly seen the importance of relationships during more than a quarter-century of building my marketing and distribution business which now reaches around the globe. Today, with a number of other companies added — from construction to manufacturing — I know more than ever that relationships are absolutely vital to anyone's long-term success.

I have always built my life on strong relationships. Whether these associations are between husbands and wives, parents and children, friends or business people, I believe we should strive to make our relationships caring and warm. Without these bonds, we are nothing but empty shells.

In fact, the most important thing you can do is to make people feel so good when they are around you that they don't want to leave you, and when they do leave you, they are anxious to get back with you. Develop the right habits, and these relationship-builders will transform your life.

That's what this book is all about — teaching people how to develop this kind of loving relationships. I just wish I could have read these pages thirty years ago!

Pastor Ross deals with the reasons why problems arise from relationships. He shares the habits we need to develop in order to build great bonds with other people. Most importantly, he gives point-by-point guidelines for putting these truths to work in our lives.

How important is his message?

Well, Jesus said we would know one another by our love for each other. Building the right kind of loving relationships shows our Christian love. That's a sign for all to see. In other words, through our ministry to each other, we actually carry out God's plan for touching the world.

I wish you all the best as you put the truths in *Seven Habits of Winning Relationships* to work in your life!

# SEVEN HABITS OF WINNING RELATIONSHIPS

*Randal Ross*

VINCOM, Inc.
Tulsa, Oklahoma

*Seven Habits of Winning Relationships*
ISBN 0-927936-50-X
Copyright © 1992 by Randal Ross
P. O. Box 65315
Lubbock, TX 79464

Published by
VINCOM, Inc.
P. O. Box 702400
Tulsa, OK 74170

**Credits:**
Editor: Larry Keefauver

# Dedication

I dedicate this book to my family, who taught me to love again.

To my lovely wife, Andrea, who is not only my best friend but who lives this book every day of her life, teaching me what it means to be a true servant of Christ. The world would be a better place if everyone were like her.

To my son, Matthew, who is bonded to my very soul. His zeal for life has made me young again. He dares to love openly.

And to Jessica, my precious daughter, whose sincere dedication to Christ and love for others keeps me on the straight and narrow and teaches me that nothing is more important than relationships. Her song makes my load light and my home a joy.

# Contents

# Acknowledgements

This book would be impossible without the help and encouragement of many people. I wish to thank David McQueen, my assistant, who helped me with research. Dr. Larry Keefauver, who not only edited and proofed this book, but kept my feet to the fire to get it done! I want to thank my wonderful congregation at Trinity Church whose hunger for truth and whose love for preaching has challenged me to do my best.

Special thanks go to Bud Housour, the vice-chairman of the board of elders, who constantly encouraged me to write and speak to the nation as well as to my own congregation. We are more than a church, we are a family.

I want especially to thank my mother and father. My mother, Phylis, who was always there, encouraging me and praying for me — especially when I was going through those tough teenage years in the 1960s. And above all, my father, Delmar. He is not only my father, but a dedicated pastor in our congregation. His encouragement, support and vision for this book were the driving forces behind its completion.

I doubt if there has ever been an author whose success depended more on others than me. I gladly acknowledge my friends — those named and unnamed — who encourage me to reach higher for the glory of God and the honor of our Lord and Savior Jesus Christ.

# Foreword

Some individuals are close to God, but removed from people. Some are close to people, but removed from God. Some are neither, and some are both. Those who are close to God and close to people are those who are most effective in life. Randal Ross is such a man.

Over the years, I have watched him in action. Rarely have I met someone with his level of relationship skills. Finally, a book about getting along with people has been written by someone who gets along with people! This book "fits right" when you read it, because it is out of the author's life, not his hip. And it proves that "we teach what we know, but we reproduce what we are."

Recent studies by Cornell University, Barna Research Group and other research firms, indicate that people skills are the most important characteristic for an employee to stand out. The Cornell study indicated that recent MBAs are quite capable of crunching numbers. However, relatively few are adept at working with people. No wonder Rockefeller said, "I will pay more for a person's ability to get along with other people than any other quality that individual might possess."

Too many people find themselves in the shoes of former Denver Bronco's coach John Ralston, who explained his departure from the team this way: "I left because of illness and fatigue. The fans were sick and tired of me.''

This book will be your guide to building healthy relationships. Randal says in Chapter 1, ''God made people for success in relationships.'' The rest of the book shows you how to be the person God intended you to be.

As you begin turning the pages, I encourage you to ponder the words of J. A. Holmes, ''It is well to remember that the entire population of the universe, with one trifling exception, is composed of others.''


John Maxwell

# Preface

My family and friends have been encouraging me to write a book for several years, but I always had an excuse. I said that the world didn't need another book writer, that I was so busy pastoring a growing church and raising a family. The excuses seemed to keep the persistent inquiries at bay and appease my conscience.

During the fall of 1991, I preached a sermon series on winning relationships to my wonderful congregation at Trinity Church in Lubbock, Texas. I had felt strongly impressed by the Lord to study biblical principles for relationships. As a pastor, I'm confronted weekly with problems that both Christians and non-Christians have with relationships. I read and studied everything I could find on relationships during my study break. I combed the passages of scripture dealing with human conflict.

What I discovered changed my life and the lifes of many people who attended that series. Many marriages were saved. Parents and children were reconciled, as we opened the Word of God week by week. But there was something else that happened: As a congregation, we began to understand the inner needs that drive relationships and how to meet those needs in a loving, biblical way.

I had originally intended to take one week on each type of relationship: marriage, friendship, parenting, etc. What I discovered was that God's plan for relationships doesn't change or vary with each type of relationship. I found something I hadn't expected.

There are only a few principles in God's Word that govern relationships. These principles apply to all relationships. When you learn the principles and apply them habitually to the core of your life, they affect everyone you touch.

As I traveled across the country speaking in seminars and churches, I occasionally shared some of these principles. The results were encouraging. I felt it was time to share them in a book.

Because of space and time, I limited them to the basic and most foundational principles. They are by no means complete. They don't cover all the principles in God's Word nor come close to plumbing the depths of God's truth. I give them to you with my sincere prayer and hope that you will allow God to touch you and lead you to winning, spiritual relationships.

God made you and knows you as no one else does. He believes in you and wants you to succeed in His will with His power. I pray that God will use these words to encourage you and give you something to help you develop winning relationships. Make them a habit, and I guarantee that they will work! God is always faithful to fulfill His Word.

These seven habits for winning relationships come from a pastor's heart to you.


**Randal Ross**

# 1
# Winning Relationships Are Important!

A friend of mine wanted to make his wife and family happy by providing a home for them. Family members each designed their vision of a dream home. To afford the dream, my friend built it himself. For two years, he worked every spare moment. Saving thousands of dollars, he constructed their dream home worth over $100,000. The week the home was finished, his wife left him. As you can imagine, his heart broke. The hardest part, he told me, was that he was doing it for his family.

My friend was sincere, but he was sincerely wrong. He didn't realize how important relationships are to genuine happiness. He thought the key to happiness was to do something wonderful for his family, when what they really wanted was a wonderful relationship with him.

Everyone wants to be happy. Everyone wants to be genuinely successful in life. This is the universal desire of all humanity. It doesn't matter if we're rich or poor, what color or how educated we may be. We all want to be happy.

The plain fact is that we won't be truly happy or successful until we have successful relationships. Winning relationships are essential for...

- Our happiness
- Our success
- Our stability
- Our eternity

## Three Requirements For Happiness

There are only three absolute requirements for genuine happiness.

**1. Security** — We desire to live with our basic needs met. We need to live life above a constant threat of collapse and failure.

**2. Purpose and meaning** — All of us need to know that our lives count for something bigger than ourselves. Down deep, we all want to do more than survive. We want to matter. We want our lives to count for something. Beyond just surviving — just making it through life each day — we need significance, purpose and meaning in life.

**3. Healthy relationships** — The final and perhaps most driving force in life is to have healthy, fulfilling relationships — with God and with those who matter most to us. Once you have successful, fulfilling relationships, the rest of life seems to fall into place. Put God first, and then others.

Happiness and success in life require these three elements. We spend our lives consciously or subconsciously seeking them.

## The Zero Factor

Without winning relationships, we'll never truly feel successful. Think of all the famous and wealthy people who have so much in life but lack winning relationships. They have much of what the world thinks is successful. But when they fail in relationships, they're not really happy or successful.

What is zero times one? What about zero times two or four or four hundred or four million? The answer is always the same: zero! Regardless of how much fortune or fame people have, they have nothing without healthy relationships. I call that the zero factor.

We recognize the zero factor in the lives of famous people such as Marilyn Monroe, Howard Hughes, Donald Trump and Jim and Tammy Bakker. As much as they seem to have, when their relationships were zero, their lives became empty and filled with failure.

Less famous and rich people have also discovered the hard way that life isn't fulfilling or satisfying without winning relationships. We need more.

Modern society has tried to take the relationship equation out of life and to fill life with things, knowledge, possessions or superficial relationships. The results are always disastrous. Life's equation without satisfying and lasting relationships keeps equaling zero.

The '70s and '80s were decades that jettisoned relationships in the search for individual, personal meaning and happiness. We sought to fill life with things, activities and events. It didn't work!

Now as we enter the '90s, there's a revival of interest in relationships. Relationships are the hot topic. Hollywood is presenting wonderful stories of people who rediscover the importance of relationships. They're learning what God has told us all along: Happiness is found inside — in relationships, not in things.

**We Need Each Other!**

Deep down in our hearts, we know that we desperately cry out for deep, genuine and satisfying relationships.

The question is: Why are relationships so necessary and important? Why do they bring us such joy and such pain?

There is one simple reason: God made us to need relationships and find life in them. We are made to need each other.

God made us to find His meaning, happiness and purpose in the midst of relationships. Even God seems to need, desire relationships to be "happy." We're made in His image, and we need what God "needs": relationships. In relationships, we find what we long for most in life.

In Genesis 1:26, God said, "Let us make man in our image, in our likeness." Strange as it sounds to our independent generation, God has made us for fellowship and to share in and rule His universe.

**God Made People For Relationships.**
**Success Is There!**

We first read of God requiring relationships in the Creation story.

> *The Lord God said, "It is not good for the man to be alone. I will make a helper suitable for him".*
>
> *Genesis 2:18*

> *There was a man all alone;*
>     *he had neither son nor brother.*
> *There was no end to his toil,*
>     *yet his eyes were not content with his wealth.*
> *"For whom am I toiling?" he asked,*
>     *"and why am I depriving myself of enjoyment?"*
> *This too is meaningless —*

*a miserable business!*
*Two are better than one,*
   *because they have a good return for their work:*
*If one falls down,*
   *His friend can help him up.*
*But pity the man who falls*
   *and has no one to help him up!*
*Also, if two lie down together, they will keep warm.*
   *But how can one keep warm alone?*
*Though one may be overpowered,*
   *two can defend themselves.*
*A cord of three strands is not quickly broken.*
                              *Ecclesiastes 4:8-12*

The Bible tells us that there is not only satisfaction in relationships, but there is God's power and presence. Listen to the words of Jesus: "Again, I tell you that if two of you on earth agree about anything you ask for, it will be done for you by my Father in heaven. For where two or three come together in my name, there am I with them" (Matthew 18:19-20).

Jesus emphasized the importance of relationships. He said that if you have a broken, hurting relationship, then leave your gift at the altar. Go and reconcile yourself to your brother or sister, and then come back and present your gift to God.

The very heart of Jesus' high priestly prayer in John 17 focuses on the necessity, power and importance of relationships. Catch what Jesus is saying: You weren't made to go through life alone. Relationships are at the very heart of God's purpose and kingdom. Without winning relationships, all other efforts will ultimately fail.

We can discover God's created purpose for relationships throughout the New Testament. Insights abound in God's Word for helping us solve relationship problems that we face daily. The New Testament contains:

- **Principles** for better friendships, marriages and parenting.

- **Exhortations** to the Body of Christ for oneness and loving one another, for cherishing and getting along with each other.

- **Admonitions** at times addressed directly to named individuals on how to correct relational problems. For example, ''I plead with Euodia and I plead with Syntyche to agree with each other in the Lord'' (Philippians 4:2).

Here is a mystery. We might think that since God made us for relationships and knows that we need them so desperately (and that relationships promise so much reward and power) that we would find relationships easy.

The truth is that relationships are anything but easy. Relationships are tough! They seem to be among life's greatest challenges and frustrations. The simple fact is that most of us struggle and feel inferior in life's most important area: relationships.

## Our Struggle With Relationships

Here are the facts:

- One out of two marriages fail. Every divorce affects at least 25 people.

- Three out of five teenagers are dissatisfied with their parents. High resentment exists between teenagers and parents.

- Seven out of ten people say they don't have a true, genuine friend. No one is there for them with whom they can honestly share, trust or feel genuinely accepted.

In the book, *The Day America Told the Truth,* more than half of Americans said they feel no one knows them and genuinely cares for them. This book also revealed that there is a growing resentment between men and women. The battle of the sexes is raging, hindering a proper respect and honest friendship between men and women. One example of how relationships have deteriorated is that some of the most common words revealed in the book that women use to describe men are dogs and pigs. Sad, isn't it?

We are perhaps the first modern generation to expect failure in our relationships. Most Americans now plan for their relationships to fail. We expect our marriages not to work, our children to have a multitude of problems and our lives to be lonely. Perhaps you know what it's like to feel like a failure and to expect your relationships to fail.

For many, we have learned to put on the facade. We pretend to have great relationships and to be happy. But down deep we know that something is lacking, that there has to be more. We feel embarrassed and confused. We don't want others to think we're failing in what we really want: satisfying relationships.

Even Christians can fail at relationships. On Sunday, we may have the appearance of having it together, but deep inside there's a holy longing for powerful, intimate, winning relationships.

Experts seem to agree on one thing: People in the world are great at tasks, but lousy at relationships. In fact, we're losing our abilities to understand and have healthy, satisfying relationships.

It's not that we don't care. It is just that we don't know how. We lack the abilities to nurture, maintain and enjoy healthy relationships.

What has gone wrong? What are we missing? Why are so many people having a hard time relating to spouses, children, friends or colleagues? Without condemning ourselves, we need to ask the $10,000 question. Why do we struggle and seem to be all thumbs when it comes to winning relationships?

## 1.   At times, we take relationships for granted.

We make the major mistake of thinking relationships are automatic. We think that because we desire them and commit to them that they perpetually take care of themselves. We mistakenly believe that relationships happen naturally — that when you want something bad enough, it will always work out by itself.

### Wrong!

Relationships never happen by osmosis. Just being with another person enough doesn't automatically guarantee a winning relationship.

One of my problems has been neglecting relationships. It's my nature to go through life quickly and alone. I remember watching a panel of older married couples at a camp play an older couples' version of the "Newlywed Game."

One wife was asked, "When was the last time your husband told you he loved you?"

"Twenty-five years ago, April 14," she said.

"Wait a minute. How do you know the exact date?" the host asked.

"I just know," she replied.

Then the husband was asked the same question.

"Twenty-five years ago, April 14," he replied.

"What happened?" the host queried.

"I told her that I loved her 25 years ago, and if I had any reason to change my mind, I'd tell her," said the husband.

Now, I'm not that bad at fostering my relationships. I seek to tell my family every day that I love them. However, I'm not good at the sloppy stuff — flowers, cards and sentimental stuff. My success in relationships is the result of hard work and a dedicated focus on others. Often, men feel as if they have many things to accomplish and neglect relationships.

Men are great at trying to start relationships and then just hanging around, hoping something more happens. They see some beautiful woman they want to marry. So they put on their best front, bring flowers, take women out to expensive restaurants, send cards with little poems that touch a woman's heart. Then one day the woman says "yes" and goes to the altar believing that the romance will last a lifetime. You know the results, ladies. Already, you're shaking your heads, saying, "No way!"

Men have a conquer-and-move-on attitude, thinking that wives and children will stay conquered by past commitment. Men move on to the next conquests, job, career, life and the world, expecting their past conquests — wives and children — to be amazed and respect their efforts to conquer new frontiers.

I call it the John Wayne Syndrome. We jump in the saddle, tilt our hats and say to our wives, "Honey, I'm going out to conquer the West. I'll be back. While

I'm taking care of the bad guys, you keep the home fires burning and the cottage clean, Sweetheart."

The woman swoons, "Oh, my man!" She waits patiently at home while her man rides off to conquer the world. If you believe that, you've been watching too much television.

Men deceive themselves into believing that broken relationships only happen to others. Some husbands take their wives out once in 25 years and can't understand why the fires of the relationship grow cold. Since they took their children to Disney World four years ago, absentee fathers can't understand why they're not close. Even attending church doesn't ensure winning relationships. No relationship should be taken for granted!

## 2. At times, relationships may fail due to ignorance.

I marvel at the number of books out there on relationships. Yet, with all the wealth of material written by authors like Dobson, Swindoll, Gothard and the like, we're still ignorant. We simply don't know how to have healthy relationships. In spite of all that's written, shown on television and broadcast on radio, we struggle with the core truths of relationships. The truth is that we often make it harder than it is.

After one of our worship services, I prayed with a woman at the altar. She was desperate for a healthy relationship with her husband. Her husband told her: "I'm happy. What's your problem?" Through the tears, she lamented, "I'm not happy. He just doesn't know how miserable he is at marriage."

We try so hard at relationships, but trying without knowledge proves futile. At times we hear James Dobson or Gary Smalley. We're convicted to have some quality family time. So we rush home, herd the family into the car and take everyone out to dinner, demanding that each person talk. Or we force a devotional time on our family that simply stresses everyone out and defeats the purpose of drawing us closer to one another and God. These efforts usually indicate that the heart is right, but we don't know how to implement God's plan.

There's good news! God's Word gives us the knowledge and understanding we need for healthy relationships. God guarantees that His knowledge of relationships is truth and will work! Without His knowledge, our relationships fail due to ignorance.

**3.  Relationships fail because we fail to understand interdependence.**

Understanding interdependence changed my life. When I learned that we are born into an interdependent world, my understanding of relationships was revolutionized. From birth we live our lives as totally dependent people needing from others our food, clothing and shelter. As we grow older, we may become sick and tired of depending upon others.

As teenagers, we say to fathers, "Dad, when am I going to have some freedom, some independence"?

The father responds, "You achieve independence when you're old enough to make your own decisions and get your own job. With your own money, you can be free to do whatever you want. Then you'll have your own life to live."

We live for the day of independence. We say to ourselves, "If we can be totally independent, then we can be truly happy!" The truth is that we're never totally independent. When we try to be completely independent, we miss God's best.

Take it from one who has been there. God didn't make you or me to be independent. Rather, we were created to be interdependent. I want you to understand the differences among these three concepts: dependence, independence and interdependence.

•   **Dependence** — This concept focuses on you. The dependent person says,

"You take care of me."
"You are to be blamed for my failures."

If we are physically dependent, we say we are disabled. If we are emotionally dependent, our personal sense of self-worth and security comes from another person. So we say to the person we depend on, "If you don't like me, then I'm worthless." A dependent person focuses on others for resources and identity.

I have elementary-age children. At times after my children are disciplined, they have come to me and said, "Daddy, I don't like you anymore." They expect me to fall on the floor in complete devastation and cry out, "I can't stand it! Please love me, Matthew! Jessica! I can't live without your love. My life is ruined."

I don't do that. Instead, I say: "Listen, Daddy loves you more than he loves almost anything in the world. You have added so much to my life. I will always love you, no matter how you feel. But you need to know that I was happy before you ever came into the world. I got along great before you were ever born. I want you to know that I love you, and I want you to love me. But when you don't, I'll still have a great day."

They look at me a little funny; then hug me; and we get on with a great life.

If you're intellectually dependent, you want someone to tell you the answers. "Give me the solutions to my problems in life. Tell me what to do."

When you or I are dependent on others, we can't function, think, feel or decide anything for ourselves. Now, independence is just the opposite.

• **Independence** — The focus of independence is on "I." We say to ourselves and others,

"I can do it."
"I am responsible."
"I'm self-reliant."
"I can make my own choices and decisions."

Independent people get what they want through their own efforts. Independent people may appear more mature than dependent people, but they still can have lousy relationships. Two independent people together can generate much soap opera material.

Sometimes, people have become independent because they're overreacting to the curse of being too dependent. Independence is better than dependence, but it leads to loneliness and conflict and misunderstanding.

God has a better way, a higher way.

• **Interdependence** — The focus of interdependence is "we." Together our lives add to each other, and we are better together than we are being independent. I bring something to the relationship, and you bring something as well. Together, our lives are better than being alone. Healthy relationships start with interdependence.

"We can do it."
"We will cooperate."
"I have been independent and nurtured, but I

recognize we can combine our talents and abilities. Life is greater together than when we go our own ways."

When we are interdependent, we realize intellectually that we need the opinions and thoughts of others. We discover emotionally that we can both give and receive love from others. Spiritual interdependence opens the whole Body of Christ to sharing God's power and joy.

Just think of what interdependence would mean to the Body of Christ if different churches started listening to each other instead of always trying to act so independent and being critical of one another.

The whole Word of God emphasizes interdependence. God made us to be interdependent. God desires that we join with one another in finding blessing, contentment, power and provision. The Body of Christ is one with many members all working interdependently together.

Paul lifts up the importance of healthy interdependence in 1 Corinthians 12. There is one Spirit and one baptism in the Body of Christ. The head cannot be the foot. If the hand says it shouldn't be in the body because it's not the head, the hand is being foolish.

What if the ear should say, "Because I'm not an eye, I won't be part of the body"? If the whole body were an eye, where would the sense of hearing be? What a serious error that would be! If everyone was like you or me, how dull, boring or even messed up the world would be! We are all members of one body — male and female, Jews and Greeks, slaves and free (Galatians 3:28). Read Ephesians 2:19-22 and 4:4-8.

As a truly interdependent Christian, I can share myself deeply with others. I have access to the vast resources, gifts and potential of other people. In the Body of Christ, we need each other. We were created for healthy relationships. In relying on one another, we find power, presence, happiness and meaning together!

Once we discover that we genuinely need others to succeed in life, we are free from the tyranny of the life of selfishness and the dead-end life of independence.

**4. Relationships fail because we have an enemy who is out to destroy all godly and potentially powerful, healthy relationships. His name is Satan.**

Satan is not out to kill all relationships. . . just the healthy ones. If your relationship is destructive, co-dependent or dependent, he'll encourage that relationship, seeking to destroy us. He wants to keep you away from healthy, successful relationships so that you won't experience the spiritual power, love, honesty, security, meaning and purpose that God intends for your life and all your relationships. The Bible says it this way.

> *"Finally, be strong in the Lord and in his mighty power. Put on the full armor of God so that you can take your stand against the devil's schemes. For our struggle is not against flesh and blood, but against the rulers, against the authorities, against the powers of this dark world and against the spiritual forces of evil in the heavenly realms."*
> *Ephesians 6:10-12*

Satan works day and night to tear apart the most powerful and precious things in the world: true, loving relationships. Relationships are spiritual. We need the whole armor of God to withstand Satan's attacks.

Information about healthy relationships isn't enough. You and I need God's help if our relationships are going to survive and prosper in these last days.

Remember, no one is exempt! Satan attacks people from every background through family, friends, church, cities and nations. I have seen 22 minister friends in the last two years get divorces. No one is exempt. Satan is attacking relationships.

You and I need God's power. When our relationships are covered by God's protection, they will succeed. Outside of His covering, we're vulnerable to attack.

We'll become frustrated if we just read the books, make commitments to do better, become more romantic or do whatever the world tells us to do for better relationships. We must have God in the middle of our relationships for us to win against Satan's attacks.

"Unless the Lord builds the house, its builders labor in vain" (Psalm 127:1). Try all you want to build winning relationships. As a parent, what will you do when your teenager gets the keys for the first time and drives off alone? Only God can protect your teenager's relationships. Only God can build your relationships with your spouse, your children, your friends and others around you.

Now, are you ready to have your socks knocked off? Before you hear all the seven habits for winning relationships, I want to share with you why all relationships fail.

There is only one reason for every relationship problem in the world! That reason is not misunderstanding, not hurt feelings, not selfishness.

All of these are symptoms but not the reason for relationship problems and failure.

## All Relationship Problems Arise From
## Needs in the Relationship Not Being Met

When needs are being met, relationships grow and prosper. But when there are unfulfilled needs, relationships become stressed.

Why do people leave churches? Their needs are not being met. Why did Sara walk out on John? Her needs weren't met. He was happy. Why do kids hit on drugs? A need somewhere isn't being met. Fulfilled needs produce healthy relationships.

I have a word of caution for you. Sometimes unfulfilled needs are not legitimate or reasonable! The needs may be real. Or, they may urgently need fulfilling. But they can't be realistically met by the relationship in which they're expressed. So if the demand for fulfillment continues to be made in that relationship, unrealistic expectations and needs can cause a breach in the relationship. The key is to find the legitimate source that can meet those needs, so that once the needs are met, a person can continue to grow and mature.

There is good news! All we have to do is identify and meet the legitimate, unfulfilled needs for relationships to be healthy. The key is that only God can help us meet the deep and genuine needs of our lives. We need God's help, and God needs our obedience and participation in His divine plan.

I have one more important insight for you.

## All Relationships Are the Same

That means that what makes a friendship work

is what makes a marriage or family work. What works in business relationships also works in church relationships. In other words, relationships are the same in essence; they only differ in degree.

As you read this book, you'll discover seven ways for making all your relationships work. You'll learn seven habits of winning relationships. These principles work in all relationships and only differ in the degree that they are applied in different areas of life: marriage, parenting, business, church and friendships.

This discovery was a great relief to me. I began studying for this book thinking that there would be a chapter on marriage, one on having little children, teenagers, friends, etc. But what I discovered was that God's principles for all relationships are the same. Learn them, and apply them to your life. They will work for all levels and kinds of relationships. It's not that complicated, and they are powerful principles.

Before you learn these seven habits, I have one final reassurance for you.

## Everyone Has Failed in Relationships

This book is for people who have had failures in their relationships. Yes, this book is for everyone.

I want you to overcome the guilt and the condemnation you have felt from failing at times in relationships. Because you have failed, or made many mistakes, doesn't mean you're a failure! There is hope. God understands our problems and our sins. That's why He sent His Son to die for us and the Holy Spirit to live in us.

You haven't failed because you are evil or unlovable or inferior or destined to fail. Even spiritual and godly people fail at relationships. Adam and Eve failed. David failed. Paul failed in a relationship with a good man named Barnabas. Even Jesus tried to befriend and disciple Judas, but that relationship failed.

More often than not, our relationships fail because we are simply ignorant. Sometimes, we just don't know how to make relationships work. We may try hard to meet the needs of others in a relationship and fail. We may have needs, and simply not know how to get them met — regardless of how hard we work at relationships.

## Give God an Opportunity

What we will recognize together in this book is that we're in a spiritual battle for healthy, winning relationships. Because we all fail, we all need help. God is willing and able to help us learn how to succeed at winning relationships. He anticipated that we would fail, and, through Jesus Christ, God did something about our failures. Jesus came not to condemn us but to forgive, heal, deliver and bless our relationships. Jesus brings grace, the power of the Holy Spirit and the Word of God to our relationships.

God is willing and able to do miracles in our lives, if we just give Him a window of opportunity. It's not too late! It's not too hard! With God, you can have winning relationships.

Your children, your marriage, your friendships can still be reached and touched. God is able.

The starting point is giving God a window of opportunity to touch your relationships. Prayer opens that door of opportunity for God to change you and others. Prayer surrenders control to God. Prayer releases faith in God through Jesus Christ to work with you in building healthy relationships. That's what these seven habits of winning relationships are all about: letting God into your life and relationships.

Before you read any further in how to have winning relationships, I want you to list and pray for people with whom you want to have relationships that you treasure and value.

List 10 people whom you cherish and with whom you want your relationship to improve:

_____

_____

_____

_____

_____

_____

_____

_____

_____

_____

Now pray. Ask God to become the center of each relationship you listed.

Read Luke 11:9-10. Commit yourself to these relationships, and pray daily for a breakthrough from God in each relationship.

Read about each of the seven habits of winning relationships. As you begin implementing these seven habits, remember to surrender daily your independence and let Jesus become your source and Savior. Open your relationships to His healing and winning power.

God cares about your relationships. Now, let's discover together the seven habits of winning relationships.

# 2

# Habit #1: Love Yourself

A teenage girl, weeping at the prayer rail in church, confides after worship service, "I hate myself." A beautiful young woman with everything to live for — loving husband and children, successful career, attractive looks, caring friends — confesses in counseling, "I think about suicide every day."

A business leader at a civic club luncheon physically looks different — changed, years younger. With a smirking smile, he whispers to me: "I just had a face lift. It's tough out there! If you look too old in sales, you'll never make it. My face lift was just another business expense."

The symptoms are all around us. Surveys tell us that average Americans may say they're handling life well. Yet, behind appearances is a gaping need in life.

## Self-love

Self-love. It's one of the most difficult and misunderstood habits for winning relationships. Nonetheless, it's a basic principle of relationships. Before we can get along with others, we must learn to get along with ourselves. To love others in a healthy way, we must learn to love ourselves as God loves us.

Few subjects are more talked and written about than self-love, self-acceptance and self-esteem. Books, advertisements, songs and conversations over coffee all focus on taking care of #1. Counselors advise, ''Be good to yourself.'' Commercials entice us to buy products that will help us be our best. Yet, the concept of self-love is not secular, but profoundly spiritual.

Self-love is biblical. Still, many misunderstand it. Some abuse it. Many fear it. There's no question that talking about self-love can become a messy subject! Some believe self-love is just another way of justifying pride, selfishness, lack of responsibility and laziness. And, at times, that's true. But the abuse of self-love doesn't lessen the importance and biblical truth that all of us need to ''get along with #1'' and ''to love ourselves.''

If self-love makes you feel uncomfortable, let me ask you a few questions.

- How can you accept others and their love if you can't love and accept yourself?
- How can you believe that others believe in you if you can't believe in yourself?
- How can others relate and get along with you if you can't relate to yourself?

Remember the story of the child who put Limburger cheese on his father's mustache while he was sleeping? The man awoke and exclaimed, ''This room stinks!'' He walked into the kitchen, sniffed around and declared, ''The kitchen stinks, too!'' Then he walked around the whole house and concluded, ''This whole house stinks!''

Desperately wanting fresh air, he ran out the front door, breathed in deeply and proclaimed, ''My Lord! The whole world stinks!''

That humorous story has a profound message. What's inside of us determines our relationships with others. Our inner turmoil, hatred or pain affect the whole world around us. Failing to recognize that we are the problem, we wonder why others misunderstand us and fail to meet our needs.

A preacher told me that he believed the problem in the world and church was that we love ourselves too much. I believe he's wrong. In spite of a generation that focuses on self-gratification, I am convinced that the problem is not too much self-love, but too little. Too few people genuinely know how to accept and love themselves in a balanced, biblical way.

Loving ourselves as God loves us isn't pride, selfishness or evil. Throughout the Bible, God commands us to release our self-hatred to His love and grace. He commands us to love ourselves. See for yourself. Read Matthew 22:37-40; Leviticus 19:18; Galatians 5:14; James 2:8; Romans 13:9; Ephesians 5:28-33.

Paul writes in Ephesians 5 that husbands ought to love their wives as they love their own bodies. That passage troubled me for a long time until I studied it closely. What Paul is saying is that if you hate your own body, it will affect your marriage. Your relationships with others are tied to your inner person — your view of self. Paul is saying that if you want to have a good marriage, you must begin with loving yourself.

Christians know that when we experience a personal relationship with Jesus Christ, our sins are forgiven, and we are changed by God's grace and love. We no longer have to hide or hate ourselves. Rather, we can accept ourselves, because Christ loves and accepts us. God's love frees us to love ourselves and others.

To hate oneself and have winning relationships at the same time is like spitting into the wind. When stagecoaches crisscrossed the Old West, Wells Fargo had few rules that made the journey tolerable for everyone.

- If you brought a bottle, you had to share it.

- If you hogged the buffalo skins, you had to sit on top in the open with the driver.

- No snoring while sleeping.

- No Indian or robbery stories when women were on the stagecoach.

- No smoking allowed, but you could chew if you spit with the wind, not against the wind!

That's exactly what the Bible is saying. If we are to get along with God, we must not resist His Spirit's work within us. We can love the self and the new creation God is forming in our inner selves.

Look at Cain, who never resolved his inner battles. In resisting God and in being frustrated with his inner self, Cain brought destruction to his family by killing his brother, Abel.

Then there was Saul, Israel's first king. His inferiority complex and rebellion against God caused such insecurity that Saul lost his son, his friend David, his family, and, ultimately, his kingship. Saul never reconciled himself to himself as a chosen, special vessel for God.

Remember Paul before his conversion when he was named Saul? So full of hate and frustration through legalism, Saul took his anger out on the church, attacking believers who were happy and joyful in Christ Jesus. People who hate themselves, like Saul, don't want others to be happy and love themselves.

To a legalist, loving oneself doesn't sound spiritual. It's too easy.

## A Warning Light Is Going Off For Some of You

"WATCH OUT!" you cry. This guy has gone off the shallow end. This sounds too much like the "I'm okay, you're okay" gospel without enough repentance and self-denial.

Listen closely. Self-love is not pride.

Pride is self-sufficiency. It is fear, grasping and groping for something that is missing.

Self-love relies on God's love.

Pride is self-centeredness.

Self-love recognizes that I can love myself because God first loved me. Self-love accepts what God says about me. God so loved me that He gave His Son for me. That must mean that I have worth and I am lovable.

Pride is false humility.

Self-love is humility without self-hatred. Humility recognizes that I am dependent on God rather than on self. When I depend on God, I don't have to put myself down!

So, when the Bible talks about being "crucified with Christ" (Galatians 2:20), I don't crucify my worth and value to God, others or myself. I die to my self-ruled, self-absorbed life. Self-denial isn't denying my worth, but denying my self-will. I choose to surrender to God's plan and Lordship, and that frees me to accept what He accepts.

Neither is self-love selflessness. Biblical self-love has its inner needs met and feels secure in Christ, so we are free to give ourselves to others. Only those who genuinely love themselves are free to focus on and give to others.

Likewise, self-love is not superiority. God has placed eternal value on each person. God made us all, and that means that none have more value than others in God's sight.

The truth is that the most selfish and self-centered people are not those who love themselves. Rather, they are those who are trying to find value and self-worth through self-centeredness.

Self-centered people say to themselves and others: "I have a bottomless hole inside me. I must take care of me before I can take care of anyone else. If I can only love myself more and do more for me, then I will be happy."

Jesus says to the self-centered person, "You must lose your life to find it" (see Matthew 10:39). Christ sets us free from endlessly seeking love, from the need to prove and earn acceptance. Those who have discovered the love of self that flows from Jesus' love are free indeed!

## Egotism Is Not Self-Love

Putting it bluntly, those who can't love themselves are egotists. Egotists are so insecure that they must continually build personal prestige up at the expense of others. They open themselves up to Satan's attack. Satan attacks egotists by robbing security, self-worth and the confidence to risk anything different or new in life. Egotists are paralyzed emotionally and begin to believe Satan's lies about inadequacy and inferiority. They are tricked — as Adam and Eve were in the Garden of Eden — to distrust God's goodness and boundaries.

Trying to compensate for lack of self-love, egotists become both self-critical and perfectionistic. Inside, they say: "If I can just become perfect, I can silence my inner voice of criticism. Others won't reject me. When I'm perfect, I can accept myself, and others will like me."

Paul tried just such a course of action. He exclaimed, "...as for legalistic righteousness, [I was] faultless" (Philippians 3:6). He tried to live a perfect, self-centered, self-righteous life according to the law. The result was dismal failure! Paul confesses in Romans 7:14-15: "We know that the law is spiritual; but I am unspiritual, sold as a slave to sin. I do not understand what I do. For what I want to do I do not do, but what I hate I do."

The answer to Paul's question for self-love — and for ours — can be found in the same place: Jesus Christ. We were meant to find self-love and acceptance in God's love for us through Christ. Paul rejoices in the freedom and self-acceptance he discovers in Christ when he concludes, "Therefore, there is now no condemnation for those who are in Christ Jesus, because through Christ Jesus the law of the Spirit of life sets me free from the law of sin and death" (Romans 8:1-2).

Satan uses our inner torment and fears to keep us from the ones who have the power to heal us and to help us. We begin to make excuses for our failures and problems. Perhaps no one demonstrates for us the damage and torment of a life without love and grace like Moses. You might identify with Moses' conversation with God and with the excuses He offered God for his self-hatred.

**Excuse #1: Since I've failed, I hate myself.**

Moses failed and had a tough time accepting himself or God's call to be someone special. God commanded him to lead His deliverance of Israel from Egypt and slavery into a land flowing with milk and honey. Moses was born with a call on his life. Born to a Hebrew family, he was raised in the royal household of Pharaoh. Highly educated, Moses had every advantage known to people in that day and age.

One day, Moses saw an Egyptian taskmaster beating a Hebrew slave. So Moses took things into his own hands and in anger killed the Egyptian. He buried the Egyptian, hoping no one would discover his crime.

We do the same thing with our sins and failures. We try to bury sin deep in our minds, hoping it will never resurface. But the Bible says, "You may be sure that your sin will find you out" (Numbers 32:23). Unresolved past sin and failure surface through self-rejection, self-hatred and running away from our problems.

Moses' sin surfaced the next day when two Hebrews were fighting. Trying to stop the conflict, Moses intervened between the two slaves, who angrily asked, "Will you kill us like you murdered the Egyptian?" Knowing his failure had been revealed, Moses fled to the wilderness for 40 years. He tried to live with self-hatred and personal failure for 40 years, keeping himself busy with shepherding, getting married and having children. Life seemed to prosper, but God intended more for Moses than simply surviving in the desert.

One day while watching his sheep, Moses noticed a burning bush. Curious, he approached the bush, and there he met God. God called out to Moses by name, saying, "I am the God of your father, the God of

Abraham, Isaac and Jacob. I am the God who called them and changed them. Now I am come to you."

Fearing God, Moses hid his face. How Moses needed God! How he feared God at the same time! Do you ever feel that way? You desperately want love, yet you still hold back, fearing God because of past guilt and failure. God is reaching out to you with forgiveness, love and acceptance, just as God reached out to Moses. He was a murderer, a failure, standing on Holy Ground. In spite of his sin and failure, Moses heard God say: "I have a call on your life. You have a mission to fulfill for My people." Moses' response was one of self-deprecation and failure.

Have you ever felt like that — like a failure, just because you have sometimes failed? Good news! God doesn't see your life as a failure! God saw tremendous potential in Moses' life, and He sees that in your life as well.

### Excuse #2: Since others have failed me, I hate myself!

Because of past failure, Moses had learned not only to distrust himself but also to dislike himself. Moses tried to convince God that the Israelites would reject him. "What if they [the Israelites] don't believe me or listen to me and say, 'The Lord did not appear to you'?"

Moses feared rejection. He'd been rejected 40 years earlier and had fled Egypt. Not only had he failed his people, Moses felt as if they had failed him. He didn't want to return to that.

You may be feeling self-hatred because others have failed and hated you. It's normal to want to blame others, but God's Word to us is that God is bigger than the rejections and opinions of others. If God is for us, it doesn't matter if others are against us. What matters

is what God says and believes about you. You're
blaming others for your refusal to love yourself. God
says to us, as He did to Moses: Go back to life, and
I'll be with you and you'll be accepted.

### Excuse #3: God, You're the reason I fail.

Moses looks at his inability to speak well in public
as a liability in serving God or loving himself. He
essentially blamed God for creating him to fail.

At times, we may do the same thing. We say to
God, "God, if You wanted me to succeed, You could
have created me with more to work with — more
talent, more money, more intelligence, better
upbringing and a better environment." Moses was
saying what we all have thought and felt at times.
"God, it's Your fault." He blamed God for making his
life harder.

God told Moses one of the great truths of life: God
makes us each different for a reason, and what we
think are problems are really opportunities to discover
God's love and blessing — if we only dare to trust and
follow Him. God says: "You can't see it now, but if
you dare to leave your self-pity behind, you'll see that
what I have planned for your life is beyond your
wildest expectations. Just dare to believe in Me as a
good God, and dare to believe in yourself.

Wouldn't you like to know that assurance in your
life? God can take your self-hatred and inability to love
yourself and transform you into a Moses — a friend
of God. Moses reluctantly allowed God to love him
and create self-love within him. It worked! God
transformed him from the inside out, and he became
the friend of God and the beloved leader of God's

people. God can work the same winning transformation in your life.

### Four Principles for Self-love: Getting Along With #1.

Let me share with you four key principles that anchor biblical self-love.

**Principle #1: Choose a single source of identity.** There can be only one place in your life or mine where we find identity, value, self-worth and self-love. The Bible says we can't serve two masters in life. We must choose between serving God and money (Matthew 6:22-24). This passage states: "The eye is the lamp of the body. If your eyes are good, your whole body will be full of light. But if your eyes are bad, your whole body will be full of darkness. If then the light within you is darkness, how great is that darkness!"

The problem so many of us have is that we're looking at too many sources to find value and esteem in life. Confusion and brokenness always come when we have too many sources of identity. What if you make a spouse the source of your value and self-love? What if that spouse leaves you, and your world comes tumbling down?

We may devote our lives to our children when they are young, but they grow up and leave. The void they leave in us can be devastating, if they are our source and our reason for living. Jobs come and go. Many professionals experience the crushing experience of losing their identity with their job.

Too many choices or sources for self-love lead to chaos and confusion. Even at our best, human beings are unreliable sources for identity, self-worth and self-love. We are all sinners, and we all let others down.

There is only one safe, secure and true source of identity: God! We are created in His image, and through faith in Christ, we are in His family. "How great is the love the Father has lavished on us, that we should be called children of God! And that is what we are! The reason the world does not know us is that it did not know him. Dear friends, now we are children of God" (1 John 3:1-2a).

Because God gives me self-worth and identity, I don't need to depend on others to give me value or worth. Now, I want others to like me. As we'll see later, they are important to God's purpose for our lives. They can add tremendously to our lives. But if I let other people determine my identity, value and worth, I'll end up brokenhearted, crushed and bruised.

So, I put my trust in Jesus Christ. He accepts me and loves me unconditionally just as I am — really am. He teaches me and sometimes disciplines me, but it's always in His infinite love. You can trust God completely. What a difference it makes when you make Him the center and source of your identity. I think that's part of what God means when He says that those whom the Son sets free are free indeed!

God's acceptance and love for us don't mean He approves of everything we do. It does mean, though, that we don't have to fear accepting and loving ourselves. I am free to love myself because God is my source of love. There is a transformation of personality and freedom that comes when we make God our source.

**Principle #2: Accept your uniqueness.** God made every one of us unique. We are a special combination of personality, experience, talents and passion. God made each of us for a particular purpose and reason.

There are times when we have the problem of comparing ourselves to others. A visitor to our church said to me: "I just moved into town, and I plan to join your church. But I want you to know that you have some really big shoes to fill."

"Great," I replied.

"My former pastor looked a lot like Tom Selleck and sang like Larnell Harris."

Now I knew we were going to have a problem, because no one has ever accused me of looking like Tom Selleck, and singing is not one of the gifts God has given me.

"Yeah, and my former pastor was so charismatic and friendly with me that we became best buddies. I just want you to know I expect much from you."

I told the visitor that I was thrilled that he'd chosen our church, but that I couldn't and wouldn't try to be like his former pastor. I was made differently, and I had to be the one God made me to be. That is the only way I can truly relate to Him and to anyone else.

I'm not saying that I've arrived or that I don't need to change. However, I've learned that when I try to be what others want me to be and not what God wants of me, I ultimately end up disappointing others and myself.

I'm reminded of a story that Bruce Thielemann tells about a man going to a famous tailor in London to have a suit made. The tailor fitted him and told him to return in two weeks. When he returned, he tried on the custom-made suit. The fit was terrible, but the customer so wanted to please the tailor that he twisted his body around in the suit to get it on. That suit completely disfigured his appearance.

Leaving the tailor shop, he got on a bus and a man asked, ''Where did you get that suit?''

''Why? Don't you like it?'' he asked.

''I'd just like to meet the tailor who can make a suit to fit such a horribly deformed body like yours,'' the man quipped.

Try living your life conforming to another person's expectations, and you'll become disfigured. You'll no longer look anything like the unique person God created you to be.

**Principle #3: Don't grieve too long over your regrets.** I believe it's time for all of us to stop worshipping the idol of our past failures. We often make gods of our failures, faults and liabilities. Each day we remember them and bow down to them. Regretting past failures, we point to a time when our lives became failures just because we failed once. We let our past rule our present and hinder our future.

We worship at the altars of what could have or might have been. The idols of our regrets and failures become bigger than God. When we allow our regrets to take control, we allow Satan to mock us, chain us and enslave us in a spirit of fear.

If I asked you right now to list all your past failures, I'd guess that, in 30 seconds, you could produce a long, memorized list of regrets. At times people say, ''Pastor, I want you to know me better.'' Before I know what's happening, they list every regret and failure from their past. They're living on past regrets.

A cartoon years ago went something like this: A terrible-looking man is sitting on the exam table in a doctor's office. The doctor says, ''My, you look terrible! Do you drink?''

"Yes, every day."

"Do you smoke?"

"Ten packs a day."

"Do you chase women?"

"All day and night," the patient confesses.

The doctor then looks at the chart and exclaims: "Your records show that you died in 1989. How do you keep going?"

"Momentum!"

Sometimes we let our past failures and problems be the driving force of our lives today, and that only leads to heartbreak and bondage. God has the answer to your sinful momentum in life: Jesus Christ! Jesus died for your sins. He went to the cross, beaten, bruised and rejected for your failures. No longer do you need to stand before the idols of past regrets. The cross has set you free!

You may say to me, "Randal, you don't know where I've been or what I've done." That's true. But I do know where Jesus has been. He died on the cross so that His blood and love can conquer anything in your past.

Remember the great speech Martin Luther King, Jr., gave on his dream of equality for all? Someday that dream may become a reality. But right now people can realize the dream to be "free at last." That freedom from past regrets comes through the blood of Jesus Christ shed on the cross. Instead of standing at the altar of your past failures, receive freedom at the foot of the cross.

**Principle #4: Pursue God's purpose for your life.** Moses wasn't really free until he left behind his past regrets and accepted his God-given uniqueness. God revealed to Moses a purpose worth living for. By obeying God's will and following His purpose, Moses discovered the freedom to love himself. When you give yourself to God's purpose, you'll be free to love and accept yourself!

I was praying for a young minister full of grief and nervousness. He had been taking tranquilizers four times a day. He confided to me: "I felt so insecure. I was so inadequate. I'd go to bed at night and pray for hours that God would give me victory over my failure."

God spoke to the heart of that young man, saying: "Stop asking Me for what I've already done for you. I died for your victory. Victory is yours if you will just start believing and moving in it."

Nothing feels quite as good as knowing that our lives are making progress — even if it's small — toward the goals and purposes God has given us. Each of us needs to hear the clear, loving voice of God that says: "I love you. Now follow Me, and discover what I have made you to be."

In 1925, the *London Times* reported the story of a little circus in London that had a big elephant named Bozo. Bozo was the star of the circus. Children loved coming around him, hugging his legs, putting peanuts in his trunk and riding on his back. But Bozo's good-natured personality began to change. The lovable elephant turned mean and angry, and finally killed two trainers.

The circus owner decided to kill Bozo. He sold tickets for people to watch marksmen shoot Bozo through the brain. Five thousand people came on that fateful day. Right before the shots were to be fired, a diminutive, balding man walked up to the circus owner and asked for a chance to show that Bozo wasn't a bad elephant.

The owner made the man sign an agreement that the circus wouldn't be responsible for anything the elephant might do to him. The man signed his name and then moved toward Bozo. The crowd stood frozen in apprehension as the small man walked toward Bozo and quietly talked to Bozo. Suddenly, Bozo shook his head and knelt on one knee. Reaching out with his trunk, Bozo encircled the man and lifted him to his back. Leaning over, the man continued to talk to Bozo. Some observers say the elephant had tears in his eyes.

As the man left, a reporter asked the man what had happened. He replied: "Well, you see, this elephant is an Indian elephant and was raised to hear the Hindi language. For these past five years, this elephant hasn't heard anyone he understood. If someone will continue to speak the language he understands, this elephant will continue to be a good elephant."

As the small man left, the reporter looked at his name on the signed agreement with the circus owner. The man's name was Rudyard Kipling. (Story retold by Bruce Thielemann.)

You may feel that no one understands you. No one loves you. You're angry, frustrated and filled with self-doubt because no one knows how to talk to your heart.

One person can speak to the language of your heart. Only one person can give you self-esteem, self-love. He is Jesus Christ. When you let Him speak the language of His love to you, you can say to yourself and others:

**I'm free to love me!**

Right now say to yourself:

The truth is that Jesus loves me.
He knows me and loves me — just as I am.
He made me for a reason. I am valuable to Him.
Because Jesus loves me, I'm free indeed to love me.
Let God's love set you free. God believes in you, and
so do I.
So begin now to believe Him, and move on in life.

# 3

# Habit #2:

# Deposit Treasure Into Others

A multi-millionaire once gave me a guided tour of his treasures. He walked me proudly around his estate, showing me his lifetime collection of paintings and sculptures. After a wonderful lunch, he then led me to his study, where he showed me his coin collection and his financial investments. After a delightful afternoon I asked him, "Which of these treasures is the most important to you?"

It would be good for each of us to ask ourselves the same question. Which one of the following treasures could you lose in life?

- Money
- Fame
- Fortune
- Home
- Job
- Church
- Relationships

I believe the most important treasure in life is relationships. Great relationships make us feel like winners. Nothing in life brings us greater joy, happiness and pleasure than healthy, spiritual relationships. Relationships are the ultimate treasure in life!

Dawn (not her real name) was an attractive young adult whose clothes reflected the latest fashions and whose presence projected confidence and self-love. Yet, as she spoke, I discovered that something was missing. Dawn spoke of an endless battle against bulimia. Looking into the mirror, she saw an ugly, fat person who didn't deserve worth or love.

Every advantage in life had seemingly been hers: money, a college education, a comfortable apartment and a car. Yet, her inner pain came to the surface as she revealed a childhood filled with betrayal, abuse, incest and abandonment. Dawn didn't have what she needed most in life — loving relationships with parents and friends.

God wants our relationships with Him and others to be treasure chests filled with joy, love and fulfillment. He wants to bind our hearts to God the Father, Jesus the Son and the Holy Spirit. He created us to live in relationship with family, friends and other Christians.

I don't know of anything that hurts more than broken relationships. I've discovered through counseling with countless marriage partners that a person can have a tremendous wealth, yet feel like a "zero" when family relationships are broken. Remember the times you've felt like a failure? You raise your kids and see them go off to college or a career. They wander from God, or get into drugs, and you feel terrible. You could say, "Well, it shouldn't matter." But it does matter, because we care. Strong relationships make us feel rich, and broken relationships make us feel poor.

Understanding the wealth of healthy relationships makes the next step an easy one. We begin to build winning relationships by learning to love ourselves and then building up others.

## Treasure Others

We'll witness one of the biggest miracles in our relationships when we put esteem and value into other people. Habit #1 is to accept and love ourselves for who we are in Jesus Christ and to take our identity from God alone. That is a wonderful and important goal. But the problem is that most of us aren't there yet. We find it difficult to accept ourselves as fully as God does.

Sometimes it's because we come from less-than-perfect relationships. Sometimes it's because we live in a world that constantly tears us down and drains our value. Some of us come from damaging relationships. Satan is doing his best to rob, steal and destroy our lives and our relationships. The issue is that we should love ourselves. We should take our esteem from God. But we're not quite there yet.

God asks you and me to build up God's people — our own lives and those around us. Treasuring others changes your life and theirs. As you develop a habit of loving and treasuring others when they're not quite where God wants them, you release God's love and value to them. It's nothing short of a miracle. The principle here is simply one word: treasuring. Treasuring is an essential habit for healthy, winning relationships. I'm setting you up for this, so listen carefully.

We don't live in the garden of Eden. We weren't raised perfectly by our parents. I don't know anyone who can raise a perfect child. The world we live in drains our self-esteem, our self-acceptance and our self-worth. We live in a world that seems to cut us down and not build us up. There seems to be such a drain in the world that continually pulls us down. Think of all the reasons why we can't love ourselves.

**1.   The world values outward beauty more than character.** If you're not good-looking, you'd better make yourself good-looking. The culture around us values beauty and outward personality more than character, loyalty and the things that really make for winning relationships. The world looks at the outside, but God tells us to look on the inside. Most of us have faced the reality that we're not Miss America or Mr. Universe. Even if you are Miss America, that beauty is for a moment. Someone better is coming behind you.

**2.   The world stresses performance.** Society makes it very clear that if you don't perform well, you have little value. The message is clear: "Your worth is directly in proportion to your performance." Your value is what you do, not what you are.

**3.   The world uses people and loves things, when we should love people and use things.** We live in a world that has a hard time defining love. They use love to keep score in tennis and to define a moment of passion with a stranger. When some tell you they love you, they often mean they want to use you.

Much too often the words *love* and *commitment* are far apart. I'm not trying to be critical; I'm just trying to tell you the way life is out there. We live in a world that is user-friendly, not people-friendly.

A woman came to me and said, "Pastor, you'd better wake up and grow up fast, because in this world — the outside world, the real world — the bottom line is that everybody uses everybody. Everyone has an angle. Everyone has a gimmick. Nobody really cares. And the sooner you realize that you don't really matter to anybody, the sooner you'll be able to handle the pain of life.''

She was talking from her own experience, and, sadly, there are far more users in the world than givers and builders. When you spend enough time in a world that uses and doesn't love, you can feel abused and of little value.

**4. We live in a world that hurts and scars us from childhood.** I was in a restaurant, and a child spilled a cup of Coke. The mother berated that child and put her down unmercifully. The mother saw me watching her and thought she'd please me by rebuking the child. ''You lousy thing,'' she chided. ''You're always making mistakes. You're never going to amount to anything!'' When I looked into that child's eyes, I saw a broken heart.

I said, ''Mamma, one day you'll regret that today in your child's vulnerability you taught her that what she did is more important than who she is. You treasure her performance more than you treasure her.''

We live in a world that is far from perfect. We need answers that are powerful enough for the real world and that can heal life's hurts. As I tell my congregation, if it doesn't work in the real world, we don't need it!

### What Must We Do to Face This Kind of Put-down, Tear-down World?

You might think it would be hard or complicated to build another up, but it's really quite simple. There come times in your life, in your child's life, in everyone's life when we need to be built up and encouraged. God's assignment to each of us is to encourage and build each other up in the Lord.

The word God gives us to build each other up is the word "treasuring." Webster tells us that "to treasure" means to place high value upon; to give great importance; to honor; to value. When we treasure someone, we might say: "You are precious." "I cherish you." "You're valuable to me." When you treasure someone, you say,

"You matter to me more than other things."
"I value you."
"You're important to me."
"I honor and need you."
"I like you. I want you to know that even if you feel like a failure, to me you're a winner."

Everybody needs someone to treasure. For many of us, victory or defeat in life boils down to having at least one person who treasures us! We all need someone who believes in us and makes us believe in ourselves. When we have someone who genuinely treasures us, it transforms us and strengthens us to a resilient life that the world's tear-down system can't destroy. A relationship based upon treasuring is a relationship that can't be easily broken apart.

The biblical picture of treasuring is really outstanding. The word *treasure* comes from the word *treasury*. The treasury was the bank in the temple of God. It was the place where God's people deposited their money to be used when needed. They would deposit an investment, building up wealth and security for future use. The more they put into the treasury, the more secure they were. A full treasury had spiritual significance for them. A full treasury brought God's blessings. It opened the window of heaven and rebuked the enemy who devoured their blessings.

A treasury is a place of safekeeping for valuables. When your treasure is full, you're not easily threatened by ups and downs of the world system. For example, if you have $100,000 in the bank, you don't feel threatened so much by a stock market that might be headed down. With a treasure in safekeeping, you can risk other investments. Without a treasure, life always seems insecure and threatening. Investing in a treasury means you have reserves that can be drawn upon for future times of need.

Here's the whole point: The principle of treasuring is that you make deposits into the lives of those around you. You value them. You build them. You treasure them and build a reserve that can be drawn from in times of attack, stress and problems. The greater the deposits you make, the greater the personal security and personal value. People who are treasured are more secure, happier and resilient when facing life's drains and problems.

Everybody has a treasury inside, and there's an account being kept. There's a place inside our hearts where treasuring and value are kept. Into the heart's treasury, God and others deposit value.

What kind of value or treasures do we deposit into one another? The coins of the treasury are engraved with:

I love you.
I value you.
You're important to me.
You matter to me.

When you begin to put treasure in somebody's life, an account starts to build from which a person can draw. So when the attacks and put-downs begin, that person can draw self-esteem and value from his or her treasury. When others have been making deposits into your treasury, you draw upon an abundance of self-confidence. When little has been deposited and your "bank account is low," it can hurt deeply. You may find yourself having many symptoms of rejection. You question your worth. You can become over-sensitive and over-reactive. Insecurity is often the result of a low bank account in the heart.

Habit #2 is simple but powerful. Make daily or regular deposits into the lives of those around you, and you'll build stronger, happier, more secure relationships. It's a principle of all relationships. Treasure what you want to keep, and build what you want to enjoy! If you want healthy relationships, just put your wealth into people.

Treasuring is based upon the law of sowing and reaping (Galatians 6:7-9). It simply says this: Whatever you want out of life, you sow into life. When you put something in, you're guaranteed a harvest. You give into another person's treasury, and both of you reap a harvest. Your treasuries build up value.

It's so simple that you might think it doesn't work — that we need something much more complex. But it does work. I've seen the principle of simple treasuring work relationship miracles.

You may say it must be hard. No, it's not. If you have people putting value, esteem and wealth into your relationship, life's hurts and struggles can be endured with more strength and confidence.

You can withdraw from your treasury into which God and others have deposited love, acceptance, strength and confidence. But when you're bankrupt and people say, "You're worthless," you begin to believe them or respond with hurt and anger. You might give up and get divorced. Or you might not talk for three weeks. Or you might go home and cry all night.

Sometimes we ask ourselves: Why do we react that way? Why do we react childishly or defensively? Often it's because we were on empty and had nothing from which to draw.

Have you ever noticed how much easier it is to go through life when your emotional, esteem bank accounts are full of love and value? The Bible is right on when it says that we should love one another, for it's the whole law rolled into one statement:

## Treasure and be strong!

### The Principle of Treasuring

If you want biblical, loving, winning relationships, then continually deposit love, value and worth into the treasuries of those around you. Now, let's get very practical. How do we treasure others? What kind of deposits can we make into their lives? How do we deposit worth, value and love into their treasuries?

Have you ever used a bank automated teller machine? Those electronic tellers are marvels of technology. You drive or walk up to the teller, insert your ATM card in the slot, punch in your secret code and enter into a world of menus and commands.

"Type 1 if you want checking. Type 2 if you want savings.... Withdrawal or Deposit?" So you punch a "2."

"Enter your deposit amount." Now you type in the amount.

"Type 1 if correct or 2 if incorrect." And so on — the chain of commands and entries seems endless.

In a way, depositing into the treasuries of others is similar. There are certain keys and actions we must take when treasuring others. Here are the keys you and I need to push if lasting, loving deposits are to be made into the lives of others.

## Key #1: Give Time and Love

You can never deposit too much love or time into another person's treasury. True treasure isn't your money first, but your time and affection. Whatever you do, don't be stingy with your time and love.

The greatest wealth we have is our time. There has been much discussion about having "quality time" rather than "quantity time." The theory says that if you're too busy to have "quantity time," be sure the few minutes you spend are "quality time."

The truth is that you can't always squeeze love and value into a few minutes. We give our lives and time to what we value, and those around us can't be easily fooled. They know by our time what we truly value.

As I am typing this manuscript, I know that I am more than a month past the deadline. Last week I injured my knee in the back yard and had to undergo surgery to repair the damage. So here I am, typing away with my leg wrapped up in a restrainer, pushing for a deadline that's already past. My daughter Jessica stops by the desk and says, "Daddy, do you want to hear my new song?" The truth is no, but I know this is important to her. She really does matter to me more than this book, so I stop and listen. We sing it together, and we laugh. It didn't take long, but it said volumes to Jessica about her value in my life. By giving my time, I said that she matters to me, and her treasury increased.

When I give seminars for both secular and Christian audiences, I tell them, "Show me your Daytimer, and I'll show you your treasure." If you want to build value in others, make them a high priority. Watch the difference it makes in your life and theirs. The more you deposit, the more success you'll have in winning, healthy relationships.

## Key #2: Surprise! Be Creative!

Be generous, not begrudging whenever you make your deposits. Find new ways to say, "I love you. You're important." When you do something special for someone, do it for no reason.

Of course, making deposits of caring on birthdays, anniversaries and holidays is important. But remember the "unbirthday" in Alice in Wonderland? There was a birthday party and gifts for no reason at all! Surprise those around you. Deposit into their treasuries unselfishly, for no reason other than to show your love. Deposits often are most valued when they're unexpected.

If you're not used to doing this, it may take a while for both of you to adjust to the new you. Remember the story of the man who was having marriage problems? He went to a counselor, who advised him to buy a dozen roses and a large box of candy. The counselor said, "Now don't go in through the garage. Go to the front door of your own house. Ring the doorbell. When your wife answers, get down on your knees and say to her, "Honey, I love you with all my heart. I want to spend the rest of my life loving you. You are my greatest treasure!"

The husband said, "I dunno. I've never done anything like that. It's not my style." The counselor assured him it would work, so the husband did as he was told. When his wife saw him on his knees with roses and candy pledging his eternal love and devotion, she began to cry.

He asked, "What's wrong, Dear? I thought this would please you."

She responded, through the tears, "It's been a bad day. First the baby spilled food on the new rug. The cat tore up the new furniture. And the washing machine is throwing water all over the basement. To top it off, you come home drunk!"

It may shock others, but when you show your love unexpectedly, it makes a large deposit! Try it and see.

## Key #3: Deposit Daily

Remember the phrase from the Lord's Prayer, "Give us this day our daily bread"? We need the deposit of God's strength and power in our lives daily. We — and those around us — also need to deposit into one another's treasuries daily. Love is something that's needed every day.

The corollary to this key is, "Don't let a treasury get too low or empty." Have you ever bounced a check? The resulting consequences and feelings are terrible. The same thing happens when we and others have nothing to draw upon from our treasuries. Life becomes miserable for them.

Children whose treasuries are empty look to the world, drugs, sex and pleasure to find treasure. Wives and husbands with low treasuries seek treasure in extra-marital relationships or burying themselves in their work. Without daily deposits, people will seek treasure, love and value in all the wrong places.

A woman confided to me: "There's nothing my husband wouldn't do for me, and nothing I wouldn't do for him. That's exactly what we do for each other: nothing!"

Make a point to do something that proves value to others every day, even if it's just a compliment about his or her clothes or a piece of fine work. Little things add up when you do them regularly.

One of the great principles of life that my friend John Maxwell taught me is that it only takes a little change to make a big difference in our lives. Little things done over time add up to logarithmic differences.

$$3 \times 3 \times 3 \times 3 \times 3 = 243$$
$$4 \times 4 \times 4 \times 4 \times 4 = 1,024 - \text{an increase}$$
of more than 400 percent!

It may seem that your situation or relationship is hopeless or too far gone. But just doing a few things differently will add up to a great new relationship. You're not that far from victory. Just deposit a little more every day, and watch the relationship grow and change.

### Key #4: Sacrifice For Others

I know this may be unpopular, but we need to face the biblical principle of sacrifice. What does sacrifice mean?

It means that we give what is valuable and significant to us to another. The Bible is clear that when we love others, we're willing to sacrifice for them and to them. It's the ultimate proof of love — whether to God or to people around us.

Treasuring gets down to self-denial. We can say and do positive things for others to deposit into their treasuries. At times, others really need to see us give up something we value for them to know and believe that we really treasure them above things and our own agendas.

When we sacrifice, the other person wins and we win. Jesus said it this way: "For whoever wants to save his life will lose it, but whoever loses his life for me will save it" (Luke 9:24). Sacrifice always brings more to the one who gives it than the one who receives it. When you sacrifice for others, you deposit into their treasury and God deposits into yours!

Jesus deposited His life into ours through His sacrificial death on the cross. When you receive His deposit, you can draw upon His life as often as you need.

There's something powerful and transforming about sacrifice. It breaks through barriers and heals hurts that nothing else can. Sacrifice is the most important key in treasuring others and receiving God's treasure into our own lives. Listen to what Jesus says: "If anyone would come after me, he must deny himself and take up his cross daily and follow me" (Luke 9:23).

There will be times in your life as there are in mine that we are forced to decide between two things that are very important to us — a long promised weekend with your family or a last-minute project at work. There are times when family members need to know emergencies happen. But there are also times when we say we're willing to sacrifice everything else because our relationships with our families are most important. It says more than a hundred cards and flowers.

## Key #5: Be Genuine

Don't be phony. Don't try to produce value and wealth in others by exaggerating your love for them. If you overdo treasuring, you cheapen what you're trying to deposit in another's life. "Love must be sincere. Hate what is evil; cling to what is good" (Romans 12:9).

Flattery is false value. It has hidden motives that want the other person to pay for the deposit. Flattery says:

"You're the best."

"You're the prettiest or most handsome."

Treasuring says:

"You did your best. I'm proud of you."

"I appreciate how you always try to dress your best."

When a father treasures his son who plays baseball, he doesn't care if his son is the top scorer, the pitcher with the most wins, or the batter with the most hits. What's important is that his son is using his God-given talents to play his best. The father recognizes hard work, appreciates a good effort, compliments and encourages his son in the midst of a hit or a strikeout.

Treasuring comes from the truth and the heart. It produces a clean harvest of genuine love and worth.

## Key #6: Treasure God First in Your Life

When you treasure God above all other things, you receive the freedom and power to treasure others.

A man called me and complained, "Now that my wife is a Christian, our entire home has changed. She doesn't love me as much. I'm getting less out of the marriage." The fact is that someone who truly values God first improves all her relationships, because she has more to give. If both people in a relationship treasure God first, they'll overflow with treasuring each other.

The two great commandments that the Bible gives us talk about treasuring in the right priority. " 'Love the Lord your God with all your heart and with all your soul and with all your strength and with all your mind'; and, 'love your neighbor as yourself' " (Luke 10:27).

Treasuring God first gives us the resources and strength we need to treasure others and ourselves. Some relationships are struggling because we haven't solved the real issue that allows God's love, plan and forgiveness to take hold of our lives. We try to solve our own problems and heal our own relationships with our own resources, not God's. If you've been afraid to put God first, let me encourage you that God first is never less for others, but more. It flows from a life that is constantly receiving God's blessings through Jesus Christ.

### Key #7: Start Making Some Deposits Right Now!

Don't wait until tomorrow to make deposits. Before the day is over, ask God for help, and then make a few new deposits.

First of all, pray this prayer: "Lord Jesus, I accept the deposit of Your life into mine. I receive You as Lord and Savior of my life."

Second, read John 3:16-17, putting your name in the blanks: "For God so loved _____ that he gave his one and only Son [Jesus] so that when _____ believes in him [Jesus], _____ will not perish but will have eternal life. For God did not send his Son into _____'s life to condemn _____, but to save _____ through him [Jesus]."

Third, make a list of the people you need to treasure more. Write beside their names what treasure you need to deposit. That deposit may be telling them more often that you love them, or spending more time with them, or deciding what you'll give them sacrificially. Make your list now.

**Name**                **The Treasure I'll Deposit**

_____

_____

_____

_____

_____

Finally, put each person's name in John 3:16-17, just as you put your own name. Pray that each person will accept the treasure of Jesus Christ into his or her life as well. Do it and watch the blessings of God flow to you!

# 4

# Habit #3: Be Genuine

"Who am I?" The headline jumped off the page of a popular woman's magazine. In the article, a wife and a mother described being a victim of the most baffling mental illness known to science: multiple personality syndrome. Forty-nine different personalities, some violent, were fighting for control of her body. Many were children. A few were men.

Her name is Vickie. She's 36 years old, the mother of three children. Forty-eight people, other than Vickie, come out at different times whenever necessary. Vickie describes her body as a glove into which each personality slips like a separate disembodied hand. Vickie never knows who she'll be next.

Interestingly, she's not so sure she wants to be free from this condition. She claims that all of these people inside of her get along with each other and cooperate. It's no surprise that her husband confesses that, at times, he's confused as to whom he's really married!

This is no game for Vickie. These personalities protect her from a violent background and childhood. In her confused state, Vickie admits that, even with 49 personalities, she's alone.

While Vickie's case may be extreme, Vickie isn't the only person on earth who lives with multiple personalities. In our own ways, most of us use multiple personalities to cope with life. Many people have different personality masks they put on to address certain problems in life. We change masks and personalities depending upon the situation we're in.

In James Patterson and Peter Kim's book, *The Day America Told the Truth,* a fascinating section is titled, "The American Nobody Knows." Some of the facts are astounding.

- One out of four people says nobody is real anymore.

- Only 13 percent of Americans say they present themselves to others as they really are.

- One out of 10 says they don't even try to be themselves.

- One out of five says that only one other person really knows them, while one out of two says no one on the face of the earth knows who they really are. Think of that: One-half of us have no one who knows the real us!

- Of those who say that one person knows them, 35 percent say that person is a best friend, while 31 percent say they are known best by their spouse. Think about that for a moment. It's scary to think that one can be married 30 or 40 years and still have only one out of three people say, "I really know the person to whom I'm married."

- Only one out of five children says their parents really know who they are, while only 5 percent say their pastor knows who they really are.

- One last finding — and perhaps the most revealing: Only two out of three Americans say they know themselves. Revealing yourself to others is really difficult when you don't know who you are!

Let me say it as up-front and clearly as I can: If you live behind masks, if you play the multi-personality game, you can't build lasting, winning, genuine, and loving relationships. You can't love something that's not real. You can't relate to a mask.

Habit #3 is vital to all our relationships. If we're going to relate to others, we must be willing to reveal our real selves, so that others can bond to the person behind the mask.

## Are You a "Low Revealer"?

Another term for someone who lives behind a mask is low revealer. Low revealers are those who don't disclose their inner thoughts, feelings, problems or joys to anyone — not those they love, their spouse or family. No one — including their friends — is at all sure what they are really like, or what they are really thinking.

At work, low revealers are skilled at small talk. But when the conversation turns to more personal concerns, they talk about the feelings of others, not themselves. They become extremely uncomfortable when the conversation turns to them. They learn to deflect the conversation with humor or banter. They are effective in shutting people out from their personal lives.

Many people are low revealers. Beyond the psychology, when you live behind masks, you're open to the deception of Satan. God is truth, and Satan is the father of lies. When you yield to his kingdom of lying, you make yourself vulnerable to the lies and manipulation of people who want to use you, hurt you and abuse you.

It's part of co-dependence, but the problem goes much deeper. Some people are continually drawn into deceptive, harmful relationships because they live with too many masks. I'm concerned at how many people who have walked with God so long can be so easily fooled by hucksters every year at the fair. They go to the fair and pay $2 to have someone tell them to knock down steel milk jugs with a weighted ball. They spend $20, and the huckster says to try one more time. And they do it!

Bar hucksters hang out to find lonely people and say the same lie that has been told a thousand times. Yet, they still draw lonely people into losing relationships. It's not just in the world, but too often in the kingdom of God. A preacher makes promises of shortcuts to spiritual discipleship and commitment. Just give to him, and everything will be easy. You won't have to belong to a group or grow up!

We get so used to living under masks and pretense that we open ourselves to Satan's lies. God promises that His genuine power and glory will come upon us when we are truly one with Him. Satan hates for people to be in oneness as God's people. Satan keeps us apart by keeping us behind masks. When we drop the masks, we can truly tap into God's power.

### Satan's Strategy

How does Satan keep us apart? He lies to us. He tempts us to live a lie. It happened to Adam and Eve. Satan came and said, "God doesn't care about you. He's trying to dominate your life. Be your own god. You can be someone different than you are." In rebellion, they sinned and began to play the game of hide and seek.

Sin broke the relationship. God came to have fellowship with Adam and Eve, but they covered up and hid themselves. It didn't work then, and it can't work now for you and me. God didn't make them or us to be phonies. He didn't make us to live behind masks. He made us to be genuine — to be ourselves.

God would walk with Adam and Eve. They would talk, and they would fellowship. There was intimacy. After Adam and Eve fell for Satan's lie, they didn't show up to meet with God. They pretended nothing was wrong. Out of that deception came a separation in their relationship with God.

The same thing happens to each of us when we try to relate behind a mask. Satan's strategy is to deceive us into believing that our real selves must be hidden from God and others. Sadly, our whole culture has learned to believe the lie.

## The Price of Living Behind Masks Is Loneliness

We're so comfortable being lied to that we expect to be deceived. Enter Madison Avenue and its hero, Joe Isuzu. Joe Isuzu was the sleazeball of advertising. Here was some greasy guy who sold Japanese cars for 30 seconds using outlandish lies. Here's how the pitch went: The car costs only $9.00 and gets 94 miles to the gallon. If you buy one today, you'll get a free house. But while he was speaking, a message was printed underneath him, warning that he's lying. Joe Isuzu's lies raised sales 21 percent in six months.

The lie that we must live behind a mask or multiple personalities has caused the top losing habit in American relationships: loneliness. Masks build walls in relationships. Masks bring the kind of separation Adam and Eve experienced.

When you can't reveal yourself to others, you become desperately lonely. Your walls not only protect you, they also isolate you. They become a prison of loneliness. You can be in a room full of people and still be lonely. You can be married and be lonely. You can be popular and be lonely. You can be rich and be lonely. You can be appreciated by other people and be lonely. Heroes can be lonely. Stars may be lonely. Loneliness is not simply being alone; it's the result of a self-made prison.

Loneliness isn't the same as being isolated. It's being walled in where no one sees who you really are. I hear about loneliness all the time from people.

"Pastor, I'm so lonely. I just don't have any friends."
"No one understands me."

So often we build so many walls, faces and personalities that someone else can't get to know us. Loneliness makes people easy prey for Satan. He works best on isolated, lonely people.

Why do we put on the masks? Sometimes we put on masks because we need to be appreciated, respected and liked. Everyone wants to be appreciated. Everyone wants to be liked. So we try to find out what people want us to be and put on the acceptable mask. But the mask doesn't ring true, so other people put on their masks as well to play our destructive games of deception.

Sometimes we wear our masks out of fear of rejection. We build invincible walls so that no one can hurt us, reject us and cause us pain. However, no one can help and love us when our house has no windows. No light, no sound, no fresh air and no people can get into our house. So what we thought would help us by making us close and giving us a secure, happy life has done just the opposite.

The good news is that Jesus has a better way! He has come to set us free, to break the prisons we live in and to touch us — the real us — with His infinite love and grace. One of the most moving encounters with Jesus was with the Samaritan woman who desperately needed to be free from her self-made prison. You can find her true story in John 4.

## Teaching a Samaritan to Be Genuine

Jesus went out of His way to meet a Samaritan woman whose relationships were in chaos. Talk about masks, multiple personalities and desperate loneliness! This woman was plagued by them all. She lived in a small town, divorced, left behind by five different men. The man she was now with didn't even have the decency to marry her. But she stayed just the same. You can imagine how the town talked. No wonder she had to be tough, she had to survive! Five times she went to the altar, and still she didn't make it in marriage.

I can see it now. Some guy dated her a few times, taking her out for dinner. He opened the car door, shut the car door, took her to Steak & Ale, bought her flowers and said, "I want to love you forever." He promised to cherish her and build her a home. Then he proposed to her. Five times she got home and found she didn't marry the guy she thought, and he discovered she wasn't what he thought. She probably thought all guys were the same: users!

In the Jewish law, a man could divorce a woman for "uncleanness," but a woman couldn't divorce the man without a great effort. So five times, some man found a reason to reject her. Five times she came to the marriage altar full of hope and joy, believing this relationship was for real. And five times she was crushed.

Now she was living in adultery. Why get married again? Just live with the guy. Why risk the shame of divorce again? She knew it was wrong, but who are you going to trust? No one commits to marriage anymore. No one is real. Life is simply using and being used.

Some of you have only been crushed once or twice. You know the pain of one or two failed relationships. Sometimes we think that our generation is the first to feel rejection and despair. But our story is as old as humankind. All of these thoughts may have been in her mind as she met a man who saw through her masks. His name was Jesus.

She had a chip on her shoulder the size of the Empire State Building, but Jesus' love began to break through her masks. He knew the real heart. Sometimes those who look the toughest and meanest are really just hurting and looking for genuine love.

As a pastor, I get to meet all kinds of people. I have a soft spot in my heart for the mean ones — the really bad ones. I love mean people. Perhaps it's because I used to be one. I understand what's going on inside of them. I love people who are angry at or hate God and can't stand Christians. I love to get to know them, because I know how it's all a mask. Many of them are desperately crying out for someone to set them free from themselves.

Jesus came to the Samaritan woman and offered her something no one else would offer. She was in a small, religious town. No one would dare touch her or get near her. She went for water in the prime time of the day when the other women wouldn't be there. But this day she found someone waiting for her: Jesus the Messiah. This Jewish rabbi communicated with her, and then He spoke to her, ''I offer you dignity. Would you give Me a drink?'' He made Himself vulnerable.

Her response was something like, ''What's Your line? I'm a Samaritan woman. You're a Jew. Jews don't ask Samaritans for anything.'' You have to understand what's happening here. Jews never walked through that part of the country. Samaritans were a mixed race that Jews detested. They were partly adulterous in worship. A good Jew would never walk through that place — much less talk to a Samaritan woman! Yet, Jesus the Messiah went there and offered this woman a conversation and a chance of dignity by serving Him.

> *The Samaritan woman said to him, ''You are a Jew and I am a Samaritan woman. How can you ask me for a drink?''*
>
> *Jesus answered her, ''If you knew the gift of God and who it is that asks you for a drink, you would have asked him and he would have given you living water.''*
>
> *''Sir,'' the woman said, ''you have nothing to draw with and the well is deep. Where can you get this living water? Are you greater than our father Jacob, who gave us the well and drank from it himself, as did also his sons and his flocks and herds?''*
>
> *Jesus answered, ''Everyone who drinks this water will be thirsty again, but whoever drinks the water I give him will never thirst. Indeed, the water I give him will become in him a spring of water welling up to eternal life.''*
> *John 4:9-14*

I want the water, don't you? Isn't that what we all want? Living water meets our inner thirst and life springs from us.

> *The woman said to him, ''Sir, give me this water so that I won't get thirsty and have to keep coming here to draw water.''*
>
> *He told her, ''Go call your husband and come back.''*
> *John 4:15-16*

Now ask yourself: Why would Jesus pull out of her such a painful experience in the midst of His healing process? Was Jesus being cruel? No, He knew the truth sets people free!

> *"I have no husband," she replied.*
>
> *Jesus said to her, "You are right when you say you have no husband. The fact is, you have had five husbands, and the man you now have is not your husband. What you have just said is quite true."*
>
> John 4:17-18

Jesus has just removed the mask! But she has another one to put on just as quickly.

> *"Sir," the woman said, "I can see that you are a prophet."*
>
> John 4:19

She's really perceptive. Notice how she has learned how to deflect this confrontation to her inner life.

> *"Our fathers worshiped on this mountain, but you Jews claim that the place where we must worship is in Jerusalem."*
>
> John 4:20

In other words, where should we worship?

> *Jesus declared, "Believe me, woman, a time is coming when you will worship the Father neither on this mountain nor in Jerusalem. You Samaritans worship what you do not know; we worship what we do know, for salvation is from the Jews. Yet a time is coming and has now come when the true worshippers will worship the Father in spirit and truth, for they are the kind of worshippers the Father seeks. God is spirit, and his worshippers must worship in spirit and in truth."*
>
> *The woman said, "I know that Messiah" (called Christ) "is coming. When he comes, he will explain everything to us."*
>
> *Then Jesus declared, "I who speak to you am he."*
>
> John 4:21-26

Jesus was doing far more than proving His deity to her. He was saying, "I know you, and I still love you. It's okay to be real with Me. If you dare to be real with Me, take down the mask. You can find the life you're crying out for!" The woman then left the water pot and went into the city and said to the men, "Come, see a man who told me everything I ever did. Could this be the Christ?" (v. 29).

"Come see a man who told me all my bad parts and still loves me and accepts me." That's what the woman was saying and feeling behind her mask.

## You Can Have Genuineness

Jesus is talking to each of us in this wonderful passage. He tells us He knows all about us, and He's come to set us free. His love and grace set us free from the need to pretend, hide or put on masks. He says to every one of us, "I want to give you living water." If you could accept that Jesus was talking to you and what that living water could do for you, out of your innermost being would flow rivers of living water. You would never be dry and lonely again.

With His living water you no longer have to put on your tough man mask or smiling mask. No longer do you have to escape to Montana and retire, never to be bothered ever again. You're free to live and relate honestly with God, yourself and others!

The Lord Jesus Christ is saying to you, "I will give you living water. But first be real with Me." You must face the "G" word.

**Be genuine!**
**Be authentic!**

For the Samaritan woman, being genuine meant honestly facing the mess of her marital relationships.

Jesus never condemned her, but only accepted and loved her.

When facing Jesus, you don't have to wear masks or change personalities. God is truth. God doesn't ask you to be perfect. The church is not for perfect people. God's presence doesn't come to perfect, good people, because there are none! The Bible says He came for sinners (Luke 5:31). He came for the sick. He didn't come for the righteous. He came to those who are lost and hurting and willing to take off their masks. That's what worshipping God in spirit and truth is all about: being open and honest — being genuine.

When I was growing up, I always thought a hypocrite was someone who smoked cigarettes in the parking lot, then came in and tried to sing in the choir. A hypocrite was someone who did something wrong during the week and dared praise the Lord and say "amen" on Sunday morning.

But that's not what a hypocrite is. A hypocrite is someone who's acting, putting on a mask. Hypocrite is the Greek word for actor. The ancient Greek plays had masks the actors would change, depending on which character they were playing. You've seen them.

The hypocrite would put on a smiling face, then go out and dance. If he acted well, the audience would throw money to him, expressing their approval. Then he would put on the sad face and go act mournfully. If he was a good hypocrite (actor) and made people cry, they'd throw more money. So the play continued as he put on one face after another.

I once heard a humorous definition of a hypocrite. A hypocrite is a teenage boy holding hands with his girlfriend in church singing, "All that thrills my soul is Jesus!"

The early church wasn't a place where people with expensive suits and impressive study Bibles would go to deny all their problems. It was a new family where they could confess their problems and love each other and be built up in the Lord. The early church was a place where love and acceptance were the chief products.

In some churches, all that happens is a spiritual show. We go and act spiritual. We put on our ''churchy'' personality or mask and pretend not to have any problems.

I was raised in a wonderful Italian holiness church. Every Sunday night, the altars were open, and we would go pray until we felt clean and ready for the world. Some would repent; others would pray for strength. But we were family there, and there was no need for pretending. We left there changed and ready for another week. Sometimes I think we need a few more nights like those days.

Today it's different. Too many Christians live behind their masks. Christians don't cry. Christians don't have problems. They don't face temptations. We come to hear the Word, worship God and go our way, taking off and putting on our masks, waiting for the applause. But down deep, something intimate is missing.

In the early church, saints admitted they were sinners and came under God's grace for healing, help, confession, and building up one another with love. True worship doesn't have a place for pretending and masks. What does the Bible say? Confess your faults one to another, and you will be healed (James 5:13-16).

Jesus is serious about this subject. He told a story about two men who went to church. One was a Pharisee, who fasted twice a week, tithed a part of his

income and prayed self-righteously (with a mask on).
Then there was a tax collector whom the Jews regarded
as the scum of the earth. There were no worse sinners
than people who cooperated with the Roman Empire
to steal from God's people.

Seeing the tax collector come into God's house,
the modern-day hypocrite like the Pharisee might pray:
"I thank God I'm not like other folks. I fast twice a
week; give a tithe; live pretty good; read the Bible;
don't beat my wife; don't curse too much."

Now the sinner stands over in the corner. He
won't even look up to God. He beats on his chest and
says, "Oh God, I'm unworthy to be in this place.
Forgive me of my sins, for I'm a sinner." Who went
away justified? Of course, the one who was genuine
and real with God (Luke 18:9-14).

The church is the place for honest, genuine
people. God knows how difficult it is for us to relate
spirit to spirit and truth to truth. That's why He sent
His Son, Jesus. The Bible says the Word became flesh
and dwelt among us, and we beheld his glory (John
1:14). In Jesus, God relates to us face to face, person
to person, truth to truth and spirit to spirit.

### Steps Toward Genuine Living

The power of being genuinely free is knowing
Jesus, who sets us free (John 8:32,36). Afraid to take
off the mask? Running to another personality?
Becoming genuine can be a scary thing at first. But it
produces a wonderful life. Let me share with you a
few principles of living a genuine life.

1. **Be honest with yourself.** When you come to
Jesus Christ, you come as you really are. As you learn
to be honest with God, you'll find it easier to be honest
with yourself and others. Remember that God knows

all about you, and He loves you even when you're at your "worst."

Since God accepts you as you are, you're free to pull down the masks, perhaps slowly at first. But you'll be surprised how wonderful it feels to be free from pretending. As you grow to know yourself better, you can live a genuine, authentic life without needing to pretend.

**2. Build windows, not walls.** Being genuine doesn't mean living in glass houses or running naked through life. The Bible never talks about being transparent. It talks about being genuine and authentic.

Transparency is like streaking. Remember when it was "in" for people to take off all their clothes and run through the public naked? Doesn't that sound stupid? A man in my church told me how he tried to streak in front of a movie theater where a big line was waiting to see Star Wars. He was stark naked, roaring in from the parking lot on a motorcycle.

The motorcycle died right in front of the line of people. He began to try to jump-start his cycle, but it just wouldn't start. So he ended up pushing it around the corner. Don't tell me there's not a fair God in heaven with a sense of humor!

When I was studying psychology at Ohio State University, they told me a few things that did stick. For example, if you can't keep your clothes on, there's something wrong with you. Now, that's both deep theology and psychology. If you can't keep your clothes on, something's wrong. People who must spill out their guts to every Tom, Dick and Harry aren't being spiritual. They're being strange.

Even Jesus Christ didn't reveal Himself completely to everyone. He was saying, "I know what's in the heart of some people and won't reveal Myself to them. I spoke to them in parables so their ears could not hear and their eyes could not see" (Mark 4:10-12).

God recognizes there were levels of relationships, and the deeper the relationship, the more windows you build to make that relationship work. It doesn't mean you have to share everything about yourself with everybody. But whatever you do show of yourself must be authentic and genuine.

## Now, Do Something Practical to Be Genuine

Do some exercises that will help you open windows in your relationships.

1. Start a journal or a diary. Begin by building windows for you and God to look through into your daily activities.

2. Share something from your journal with a friend or spouse. You don't have to share everything. Initially choose something that's non-threatening. Then proceed from there.

3. Find someone to be your prayer partner. When you pray with and for each other, begin sharing honestly. Confess your sins and your needs as you are led by God's Spirit. Prayer is a great way to grow together honestly and with integrity.

4. With your family, make being genuine fun. Have activities in your family begin to build little windows. My family plays a game when we go to a restaurant or gather around the table. We start with fun questions. "What's your favorite color?" Later, we may begin to reveal more deeply about ourselves.

"What's your greatest fear? Who's your boyfriend?"

I've discovered when I talk to people that not one out of 10 couples who've been married more than 20 years know their mate's greatest fears and temptations. Spouses can rarely tell me their spouse's greatest joy and hope and desire.

If we don't build some windows, we won't have lasting, deep, winning relationships. Start by asking the right questions, and make it fun.

5.   Turn off the television. Watching television together is not being together. Begin talking with one another. Go for a walk. Have a cup of coffee together. Learn about each other at a normal pace.

6.   Spend time with Jesus Christ. There's only one person with whom you can be totally genuine, open and transparent: The God who loves you and made you. He knows you, good and bad, inside and out. He says that if you come to Him and want His presence, power and vitality, just open up and be genuine. You don't have to be perfect. But stop acting, being a hypocrite, wearing your masks. You can't lie to Him.

Confess your sins. Open your heart, and let the healing power of Jesus come through your open window. Be genuine and discover the reality that the Samaritan woman found. Allow people to relate to the real you. God says that the real you is worth knowing.

So let's start building some windows!

# 5

# Habit #4: Commit to Others

Years ago I heard the story of a child taking his first cross-country train trip. In the sleeper car, the mother, father and boy were preparing for sleep. Everyone was tucked in behind those Pullman car curtains when the child anxiously asked, ''Dad, are you there?''

''I'm here. Your mom's here. And God's here,'' reassured the father.

A few minutes later, a second inquiry came. ''Mom, are you there?''

Patiently the mom answered, ''Yes, son. Your dad is here. I am here. And God is here.''

A few more minutes passed, and the child asked again, ''Dad, are you still there?''

A man trying to sleep in one of the other bunks answered this time. ''Yes, your dad is here. Your mom is here. And God is here.''

With some awe and a little apprehension, the child hesitantly asked, ''Dad, was that God?''

Every one of us deeply needs security. When we lack security, we're plagued with self-doubt and unstable relationships. One of the major symptoms of insecurity is fear: fear of loss, fear of failure, fear of being let down. Insecurity affects our relationships as few things can. It's almost impossible to have a happy, fulfilling relationship when you feel threatened or insecure all the time.

Insecurity is a national plague. We search high and low for something or someone to make us secure. But we usually come away feeling that something deep inside is lacking. It's an inner hunger that drives us to often tragic results. We begin feeling as though nothing we do is enough to accomplish our goals.

One man said to me, "I have this feeling that I'm going to blow it and lose everything. I don't know what to do about it." He's been through several marriages and has changed jobs 10 times in the past 20 years all in search of security.

Insecurity is a cancer to winning relationships. When we feel we're on "thin ice" or insecure, it's hard to truly give ourselves to that relationship. The $64,000 question is, Where can we find security? What has the power to produce security in those we love and bind us together in a tear-apart world?

Here's the key. If we can find the true source of security, we'll find the stability and confidence to build winning relationships that can last the storms of life. That's the purpose of this chapter: To find and release the true source of security in your life and in those you love. Then you'll be able to build winning relationships.

## Searching For Security

In Mark 10:17-30, we meet a successful man who was looking for more. He seemed to have everything in life. But something was missing deep inside. In one sense, he could be considered the original baby boomer. The encounter goes like this:

> *As Jesus started on his way, a man ran up to him and fell on his knees before him. "Good teacher," he asked, "what must I do to inherit eternal life?"*
>
> *"Why do you call me good?" Jesus answered. "No one is good — except God alone. You know the commandments: 'Do not murder, do not commit adultery, do not steal, do not give false testimony, do not defraud, honor your father and mother.'"*
>
> *"Teacher," he declared, "all these I have kept since I was a boy."*
>
> *Jesus looked at him and loved him. "One thing you lack," he said. "Go, sell everything you have and give to the poor, and you will have treasure in heaven. Then come, follow me."*
>
> *At this the man's face fell. He went away sad because he had great wealth. . . .*
>
> *Peter said to him, "We have left everything to follow you!"*
>
> *"I tell you the truth," Jesus replied, "no one who has left home or brothers or sisters or mother or father or children or fields for me and the gospel will fail to receive a hundred times as much in this present age."*
>
> *Verses 17-22,28-30*

This young man's hunger teaches us much about life and security. He had what the world says produces security: money — lots of money. He was a good young man, doing his best to serve God and to find spiritual peace. But something was lacking. He didn't really feel secure. Something was missing.

So he went to the one who had everything he longed for. Jesus gave to him and to each of us the fourth principle of winning relationships. It's as relevant today as it was 2,000 years ago.

I'm convinced there are more miracles and ability in this fourth habit than any other we'll explore together. Listen to the *Saturday Evening Post* in an open forum column. I'll leave the word itself out and see if you can guess it.

*It is a big word full of big promises for those who take it seriously. It's just a quality something you can't see or feel, but it is a fact of life. All your goals, dreams, ideals and hopes in this world fade away without this vital ingredient.... There are many roads to success and happiness, but none will get you there if you don't take this one along as your walking stick.*

What word are we talking about? What's the one thing that releases such power and blessing in our lives? Something that even the secular society recognizes. The article hits upon a vital truth to our relationships. There is a principle here not to be neglected, and it's essential to everything in life.

I don't know how you were raised, but some of us were raised in churches hearing sermons that taught us to feel insecure with God and therefore with others. I don't believe that approach was malicious. But too often it instilled within us the root of all insecurity. If you feel insecure with God, you'll usually feel insecure with others. If you believe God who knows you best would let you down and turn you away, then you expect others to do the same. It produces a deep insecurity that follows us throughout life.

That is not God's will for His people. It is not His will for people to be insecure or unstable with Him or others. It is a plague on the Body of Christ.

God sent His Son to make you feel secure, and He wants you secure in Him. He wants you resting in Him. He wants you to know He has resources. He loves you. For when you are insecure, Satan can deceive you and lead you away from God and those who truly love you. Satan takes spiritual insecurity and leads us to a wasted life looking in all the wrong areas for security.

If we continually hear how God will punish or reject us every time we fail or step out of line, we begin to look for security in other places. Everything good begins with God. When our relationships are right with God, we're free to make it right and stable with each other.

We're slowly learning what the rich young ruler discovered. Money and religion don't make you feel secure. God does! Religion — human attempts to work things out through self-righteousness or perfection — makes us feel insecure. For no one can be justified or feel secure by the works of the law. Our works are never enough.

Religion will never make us feel secure. Going to church will never make us feel secure. Giving our tithes won't make us feel secure. Reading our Bibles won't make us feel secure — if we fail to fill in the void in our lives with a personal, secure relationship with Jesus Christ.

Relationships make you feel secure. That's it. In secure relationships, you find joy and peace and love. When you feel secure in your relationship with God, with your wife or husband, with your kids, with your friends, you don't have to waste your life looking in all the wrong, dead-end places for security.

You're probably saying, "Enough already!" What's the word, the principle that produces security with God and with others? It's the "C" word.

## Security Is Built By Commitment

There's one solution to most of our insecurity. The fourth habit of winning relationships that God gives in His Word is commitment.

Surprised? Disappointed? Before you turn me off and close the book, let me explain. Most of us don't understand commitment. I don't know of any other word in the English language that has more power and potential, yet is more misunderstood, more feared, more avoided, and produces more guilt. But without commitment, you don't have secure relationships.

That's the bottom line. Think about it. Children are insecure when they don't feel commitment from parents or other important people. Your spouse is insecure when he or she doesn't feel commitment in the marriage relationship. You feel insecure when your colleagues or friends don't demonstrate commitment to you.

One of my new staff members asked to speak to me in private. As he shut the door, he looked straight into my eyes and said, "Pastor, what happens when I fail? Will I be fired or demoted? I have to know. The suspense is killing me."

I put my arm around his shoulders, looked straight into his eyes and smiled. "Don't worry. You've already made a dozen mistakes, and you're still here. It's okay. You're part of the family, part of a committed team."

Commitment produces security. Where there's no commitment, there are no secure, winning relationships. Everyone has to have a regular dose of commitment to survive life and build healthy relationships.

Now, I know we're in the "hang loose" generation. Commitment is "out." Flexibility is "in." We want to hang loose and keep our options open. Commitment is today what "I love you" was to John Wayne. He loved his horse, but he kept very loose and free with everyone else. The ideal of personal freedom has blinded us and robbed us of one of the most powerful habits and principles in life: loving commitment.

Today's society is paying the horrible price of life lived without commitment. Our generation goes to great lengths and rationalizations to avoid commitment. Commitment today is what "I was wrong" was on *Happy Days*. Remember, Fonz never could say it. We're the same way with commitment. We're just so afraid of it.

Why are we so afraid of that word? Why do we hate it? Why are we so nervous and avoid commitments, when we know that they're part of God's plan for our life? Let me show you a few reasons why we struggle with commitment.

**1. Fear** — At times we're afraid of commitment because we fear we'll miss something in life. If we commit now, we might miss something better when it comes along. Yet, we are so bound up in our fear that everything keeps passing by us.

**2. Failure** — Since we have failed in past commitments, we avoid future ones. Sometimes we avoid commitment because others have failed us when they made commitments. We become tentative in our relationships.

Bob and his family experienced losing relationships in a church that had a warped view of discipleship and commitment. Now he and his family struggle with entering fully into the joy of a genuine, loving church. So he sits in the balcony, always feeling out of place. We can understand how he feels and why it's hard. Still we hurt for him, because we know his past is robbing his today of a joyful life.

Our past failure makes us cautious about present commitments, because we don't want to be hurt, disappointed or discouraged again. Experiences have taught us that people who make commitments to us can sometimes let us down.

**3. Ignorance** — We simply don't understand or know the power and meaning of true commitment. We don't know how to make or keep our commitments. Far too often we've bought into the false promises of personal freedom, just as the rich young ruler did. Far too often relationships fail, not from desire but from ignorance.

**4. Lack of desire** — Then, we may simply lack the desire to make a commitment. We can't find anything or anyone worth the genuine sacrifice of commitment. We've been blinded by a world that tells us that even God will let us down, so we need to be free of all commitment to find true fulfillment in life.

As I researched this subject, I talked with my friends. Many of my fellow pastors lamented to me that no one wants to commit anymore, and they had impressive statistics to back them up. The signs are everywhere that no one wants to commit anymore. It's common knowledge among the general public that 50 percent of marriages performed this year will end in divorce within five years. Think about it: One out of two people married in America this year will be divorced in five years. Sixty percent of the children raised in this generation will be raised by a single parent. That's too much insecurity being produced in our society.

Church attendance is increasing, but few people want to join the church anymore. It gets harder and harder to get people to sign on the bottom line, to limit their options. I'll admit that commitments are harder to come by in the '90s than any time I can remember in my years of pastoring.

But I don't believe that, deep down, we genuinely resent commitment! I don't believe that. I believe people desperately crave commitment. That's why the cults are growing so rapidly. They offer commitment and community. They produce commitment — even if it's to the wrong things.

There's an intense hunger for commitment in your life and mine. That's the way God made us. The question is, Where do we find someone who will commit to us, anchoring our lives amid the ever-changing storms of life?

I believe there's such a hunger for commitment down deep in this generation. But our energies are being channeled into all kinds of destructive things. Think of the Los Angeles riots in 1992. It appeared to many Americans that our legal system failed in its commitment to protect Rodney King from police brutality. Like a string of dominoes, first commitment to justice seemed to fail, then came the rapid fall of commitment to decency, law and order, respect for personal property and civil rights. Our fragile commitments fail us, and society comes unglued.

The answer is the same answer Jesus gave to the rich young ruler!

## Commit to the One Who has proven His commitment to you!

In effect, God says, "I know your fears, and I know how you feel. So to prove My love to you, I commit to you first so you can be free to commit and follow Me." Listen to the words of Paul to the church at Rome:

> *You see, at just the right time, when we were still*
> *powerless, Christ died for the ungodly. . . . God demonstrates*
> *his own love for us in this: While we were still sinners, Christ*
> *died for us.*
>
> Romans 5:6,8

When we truly see God's commitment to us, we're free to commit genuinely and fully to Him. Once we're at peace with God and at rest in Him, we have the freedom to commit to others and trust their commitments to us.

Commitment changes your life. It works miracles when you dare to commit. Commitment is God's way of releasing His power and security in your life. Here is what the Bible says.

Psalm 37:5 reads, "Commit your way to the Lord; trust in him and he will do this." Then in 2 Timothy 1:12, we see, "Yet I am not ashamed, because I know whom I have believed, and am convinced that he is able to guard what I have entrusted to him for that day."

Commitment is the habit that produces security in your relationships. Commitment is the principle that releases the potential you have into reality. The absolute way to fail in life is to avoid commitment. I know committing can be scary, but, as you begin to see the results, you'll take the risk!

A successful businessman and friend, Art Williams, confirms that the surest way to failure is to lose the ability to make a commitment. Lack of commitment, he says, causes many business failures and career failures. Failures are due not to a lack of skill, lack of talent, or even lack of hard work. Rather, the failures result from a lack of commitment. Art tells me that some people work and work but seem to spin their wheels. They're often missing the vital ingredient: total commitment.

Art once hired a very capable woman named Carol as a sales representative for his company. A college professor, she wanted to increase her earning potential and gain the opportunity for a sales career.

Ten months later, she came back to Art's office, exhausted and totally discouraged. She was working furiously, making calls and seeing clients. But she was getting nowhere.

At first, Art couldn't recognize her problem. Obviously active and smart, she was making an impressive effort. Then she told him she'd taken a one-year leave of absence from the college. She had only two months to decide whether she could make it in sales or lose all her benefits from the college if she didn't return.

That was her problem! She hadn't made a total commitment to her new work, and it was showing in her performance. She knew she could return to her teaching job if she couldn't make it in sales. She thought she was holding a trump card, but it was holding her. Art gave her a choice. She had to go out on a limb. She had to choose between giving up any thought of returning to the college, or she had to return to her safe job.

Not only did she make the decision, but her whole family moved. Three months later, her income tripled. In one month, she made more than in one year of teaching. Three months later, she was promoted to an executive position within the company. Commitment made the difference between success and failure.

## Commitment to Christ Anchors
## All of Life's Commitments

If you're not committed to God's plan for you, you'll never truly experience the life God has for you. In one sense, you bring failure upon yourself. That's exactly what God has been telling us in His Word all along.

"But when he asks, he must believe and not doubt, because he who doubts is like a wave of the sea, blown and tossed by the wind. That man should not think he will receive anything from the Lord; he is a double-minded man, unstable in all he does" (James 1:6-8). A double-minded person receives nothing. A double-minded person who isn't committed to one thing and one task receives nothing out of life.

You may think you have an escape hatch by hedging on your commitment to God. But actually, it's a noose, killing God's blessing on your life.

That's why some believers' finances are so messed up. They refuse to commit all their resources to God. They want to keep their options open. They want to try giving or tithing for a while, but think in the back of their minds that they can quit whenever times get rough. God wants our single-minded commitment. He wants us first to seek the kingdom of God and receive His blessing. It's not the money, but the spirit of commitment and trust that brings God's blessings. That's what Jesus is telling the rich young ruler: Dare to trust Me. Dare to commit and follow Me. And the life you hunger for will be yours — guaranteed!

Hebrews 11:6 reads, "And without faith it is impossible to please God, because anyone who comes to him must believe that he exists and that he rewards those who earnestly seek him." Can you see how

Satan robs our relationships, our finances, our minds, our jobs, and our eternity by making us double-minded? Satan uses double-mindedness and lack of commitment to bring us back into subjection and bondage.

Remember the end of the story of the young ruler? The inquirer turned away from Jesus. He wouldn't commit. He understood. He knew Jesus loved him. But he just didn't take the leap. When he failed to commit, Jesus moved on, and he was left behind. He let his fears — perhaps his experiences — rob him of real life, a personal, intimate relationship with God.

Notice this: We've been taught that low commitment is adequate for the power, resurrection and life of Jesus Christ. I wish it were true, but it's a lie from the pit of hell. What was true then is true now. Either you're committed, or you don't have eternal life! You don't add Jesus to your life. You commit totally to Him. Jesus says that unless someone dies to self and lives for Him, that person can't follow Christ.

I must have come to the altar 500 times when I was a child. Every Sunday I got "saved." My dad was the preacher. Time after time, I would come down and pray with my dad, saying: "Oh, Lord, I'm sorry for my sins. Lord, forgive me. I don't wanna go to Hell. I don't wanna go to Hell and burn with the crispy critters. I don't wanna go down there with Hitler and Mussolini. I don't wanna go down there. Lord, forgive me. I don't wanna perish. I'm afraid, and I repent and take Jesus."

By Tuesday, it was forgotten, and the commitment was gone. Some of you have been on the same guilt trip of confessing on Sundays, but not really committing.

I lived for years without a true commitment. When I was 20 years old, I hit bottom. I came to the altar and said: "Jesus, this is it. I'm tired. I'm tired of You bothering me. I'm tired of being on the fence. I need relief. I need something that works! I don't like You. Matter of fact, I'm about ready to go to Hell. Lord, just to be relieved of the torment, the insecurity, the frustration and the fear of failure, I surrender all. Okay, Lord, it's everything. It's my reputation. It's my friends.''

What a difference it made! Everything in my life changed instantly! What a difference the "C" word — commitment — made! I stopped being double-minded. I walked out a different person. Commitment — surrender — makes a difference! It unlocks the door to God's miracle-working power.

Remember Jesus' parables about a man finding a treasure buried in his field or a pearl of great value (Matthew 13:44-46)? In each parable, the central characters make a total commitment to obtain the object of value. Neither one turns back nor questions the need to do everything necessary to make the purchase.

With the rich young man, the merchant and the man buying a field, Jesus says commitment is the key to a relationship with Him. As long as you have bridges to walk back on, you'll never be powerful in Jesus Christ.

Always got a bridge for an escape? Someone hurts your feelings? Something doesn't go right? Someone embarrassed you? Feeling like dropping out on your commitment to Christ? Stand firm!

If you submit to God — that means commitment to God — you can resist Satan. Satan has to flee (James 4:7). But don't bother rebuking the devil and challenging evil if you're not committed and submitted to Jesus Christ. Submit to God, then you can resist Satan.

Commitment is not just a principle for your relationship with God. It unlocks the power of security in all relationships. It changes your children, your spouse and you. Commitment transforms relationships by meeting the deeply felt need for security.

Here's how it works. Every relationship is no stronger than your commitment. Go to your children, look them straight in the eye and say: "You will make mistakes in your life. I did, and I still do. I want you to know that I not only love you, but I'm also committed to you — 100 percent forever! Nothing you can do will stop me from loving you! Now we may have disagreements, and I will discipline you in love. But I will always be there for you!"

That changes your child! Do it with your husband, your wife, your friends, and it will release others to commit to you.

Want to stay married? Commit to your spouse for better or worse — and mean it. Want your kids to be secure? Quit fighting and talking about divorce in front of them. I know it hurts and that it's hard. But life is hard on those who don't release commitment.

The deeper the relationship, the more commitment it takes. That's the price you pay for powerful relationships. But the good news is that the joy of the relationship far outweighs the cost!

### Commitment Has a Price Tag

There's a story about the chicken and the pig who belonged to a struggling farmer. The chicken said, "Let's help the farmer out by giving him breakfast. I'll give some eggs, and you can provide some bacon."

The pig responded, "That is easy for you to say. You're just making a contribution. For me, it's a real commitment!"

I'd like to tell you commitment has been easy for me since I became a Christian. But that's not true. I was afraid to get married. I enjoyed being single. I was a great single. When I thought about marrying this lady (now my beautiful wife), I thought my life and my freedom would be over. I wouldn't be able to go out with the guys. I was scared, but I knew the commitment would be worth the sacrifice.

When I woke up that first morning of our marriage, I said, "You know, there's going to be somebody in my bed taking up my space the rest of my life!" The person who said the first two years of marriage are the honeymoon — the best years of your marriage — should be taken out and shot! Our marriage was horrible! We fought all the time. I missed my freedom. I was afraid.

When people ask what kept us together, I tell them one thing. I made a promise to God never to go to sleep angry or fighting with my wife. I've kept that promise for 18 years now. Sometimes those first few years I might not have slept for three days. But I never went to sleep angry at my wife. Eventually, I was tired enough to patch things up and to apologize. The "C" word got us through. I'd like it to sound more spiritual, but I don't think it's the feelings or goose bumps that get us through the hard times. It's commitment. I'd made a commitment for a lifetime.

Then came the parenting commitment. I never was happy about having kids. First, we didn't want them (my wife says she did), then we couldn't have them. After our first child was born, I got this little thing that was throwing up and keeping me up all night long. I asked, "How many weeks do I have to put up with this?"

And the doctor said, "Weeks?" You're talking decades, Son. Decades." Now I get an allowance after my kids get all the stuff they need. I asked my wife, Andrea, "What about me?" She replies, "That's the way life is, Buddy. You're a father now." Sometimes I don't get the things I'd like. But the joy of those two children far, far outweighs the cost of commitment.

Seriously, the next best thing to Jesus Christ and my wife is having my children. Now, children are a commitment. They are expensive and they take up time. They're always on me, asking, crying, wanting, needing, talking. They won't let me sleep or study. They're pulling on my shirt and wanting to wrestle. Always wanting to eat — four or five times a day. Milk just goes.

What's the bottom line? It's worth it. Commitment to Jesus, to a spouse and to children — all are worth it!

## What About My Broken Commitments?

Some of us are unwilling to make new commitments because we've failed in past ones. Remember, I told you that every one of us will fail in relationships. That's why Jesus died for us. I want you to know that there's a practical way of handling your grief and fears of broken commitments. Before you go on — right now — handle your broken commitments. How?

• **Admit and confess them.** Don't hide them. Guilt and sin hold us as long as we hide and deny. Get it out in the open where God can heal you and set you free.

- **Don't blame others.** Accept responsibility for your part in the failures. Blame only adds to the problem. Take personal responsibility for what you did wrong.

- **Pray.** Ask God's forgiveness, and seek the forgiveness of others.

- **Make restitution** where at all possible and where the restitution won't bring further pain to others.

- **Then, let the failures go.** God forgives you. Forgive yourself! You don't have to let your failures destroy your today and tomorrow.

The pathway to security in your relationships begins with commitment. God is calling you to commit your life to Jesus Christ. Burn your bridges of excuses and doubt. Release the power of God in your life, and experience His miracles in your life.

Renew your commitments to family and friends. Tell them and show them how much they mean to you. Take the following steps now:

1. Commit yourself to Jesus Christ as Lord and Savior.

2. List those you need to ask for forgiveness from past, failed commitments.

3. Now list those people you'll go to right now and renew your commitments, expressing what you will do. Then do it.

4. Let God's forgiving love set you free from the past and begin His miracle-working power now in your life.

**Dare to sign up now! It's worth it!**

# 6

# Habit #5:

# Release Past Guilt and Failures

Some relationships win, succeed and prosper. Others fail miserably. In the same week, I encountered both.

A couple came to me and the husband said: "Pastor, I have to tell a testimony. I don't belong to your church; I'm from a different faith. I was driving down the freeway on Sunday morning and got in the wrong lane. I was forced to the exit ramp at University Avenue leading directly to your church. So I said to myself, 'Well, I'm here and the traffic is going that way, I may as well go to church.' My car ran out of gas in the parking lot."

The man told how he walked in and sat down in the back of the service. He saw a drama about a husband and wife fighting. He and his wife had been separated for quite a while. As he watched the drama, he thought, "Wow! That's exactly what has happened in our marriage."

He came back to church that night for the worship service. Then he said, "You know, Pastor, I was just worshipping God, and suddenly I felt this warm presence of God. I think that's what you mean by being filled with the Holy Spirit. It was so wonderful because I knew that God had touched me.

"I looked as I went out the door, and I saw my wife's car. She was in the service, too! I felt God say to me to go and talk to my wife. I told God, 'Hey, God, You don't know my wife. She won't talk to me. We're at each other's throats. If she knew I was here, she'd walk away.' God said, 'Go talk to her.' "

The husband went over and talked to his wife. At first she refused to listen, but she decided to give him 10 minutes. The next Sunday they were in church together, sharing a marvelous testimony of how God restored their marriage and got their marriage back together. He said, "Oh, it's been so wonderful." They had renewed their commitment to each other in the church parking lot.

I was touched by that testimony, but I've also received phone calls and letters from people who are struggling with failing relationships.

During the same service that this couple shared about their exciting reunion, I prayed with another man at the prayer rail. His story was just the opposite. For months, he and his wife had been fighting and moving further and further apart in their marriage.

Painful accusations continued night after night. They had tried counseling, prayer and read numerous books about marriage. Still, no relief was in sight. He asked for prayer, because the next morning he would be moving his things out of their home of 15 years and into an apartment. Tears streamed down his cheeks. He wanted the marriage to work. He was committed to his wife and loved her. Both had tried their best. But something still wasn't working.

Perhaps you're in that predicament. Things aren't going well at times, and you're having losing relationships. Maybe you've tried your best, and you've had to come to a painful awareness that relationships don't always work out the way you'd like.

At times, relationships may fail because we don't try or we're not committed. But other times, relationships fail even when we try our best and we want to be committed. In fact, as I wrote earlier in this book,

**Everyone fails at relationship some
time in life.**

You won't win in every relationship. Relationships get broken, even when you try your best. That's the hard side of life, but it's one that must be faced honestly. I want to talk about why relationships fail, what to do when they fail, and how to handle it. In Luke 15, Jesus told the parable of a prodigal son and a loving father. It's my favorite story in the whole Bible, and I want to reflect on that story with you.

## Letting Another Person Go

The father represents God. He had two sons. He loved those kids. He existed for those children. He wanted them to prosper and eventually take over the farm. He wanted them to have everything their hearts desired. He wanted intimacy and relationship with them.

He gave his life for those two kids. But all was not well at home. The youngest son had an attitude. He was a cruel child. He demanded his inheritance before the father died. It would have been his eventually, but he couldn't wait. By his actions in demanding his inheritance now, he simply said: ''Dad, you're dying too slowly, and I want it now. Give me my inheritance. I want to go away and have my own life.''

Amazingly, the father agreed! The son got what he wanted. If you're a parent, you can see what's coming. We cry out to the father, "Don't you know that the kid will blow it? Don't do it; don't let him waste it!"

But the father divides his inheritance with his son. It wasn't long before the son took his money and left town. Sure enough, he blew it, squandering it away and ruining his life. He reached bottom.

Then something clocked inside the young man's heart. The Bible says he came to himself and decided to go back home. Then there's one of the most moving reunions in all of scripture, as the father rushes to meet and restore the broken son. It took courage for the son to admit he'd made a mistake.

I remember going to college and finally getting away from the restrictions of my father and mother. It seemed to me that they went to church all the time. I just wanted to be free — to be my own boss. I said, "Mom and Dad, I've been living for this day. I don't need you, and I don't need God. I have a scholarship. I'm on the top of the class. I'm going to make something out of my life, and I'll prove it to you."

I lived the prodigal son story.

To understand this story, though, you have to know that the story isn't about the prodigal son alone. It's about the father and one of the great principles of relationships. Can you understand that he gave his child wings?

After he did all he could do and influenced all he could influence, the father knew that the child had to make a decision. He decided to go away, and the father said, "I love you enough to let you make your own destiny. I love you enough to let you go!"

Parents know that letting a child leave isn't easy to do!

People say to me once in a while: "Pastor, why is there AIDS, starvation, warfare and death? Why is there all this mess in the world? If God is so good and God is so loving, why do people hurt so much? Why is there so much divorce and all the garbage in the world, if God is so loving and God is so good. Why does He allow such suffering and pain?"

It's because God has given us a wonderful and awesome gift. It's the gift of personal choice. It's called free will.

You know how it works. God says: "I love you too much to make you a robot. I don't want robots. I want those who choose to relate to Me and to love Me of their own choice. I don't want slaves, because slaves can't be friends. And robots have no personal response. I made you with the freedom to choose. I'll let you choose your own destiny. Choose Me or reject Me. Choose heaven or choose hell. Choose life or choose death. But remember, I love you enough to let you live by your choices."

It's significant to me the father in the parable didn't run after this boy. He didn't chase him down. He didn't bail him out of jail. He didn't post bail. The father loved that boy, but he knew he'd never have that son back if the son didn't choose the relationship.

The miracle is that the father gave wings to his son and let him go. So when the boy came to himself and realized he was mistaken, he did what I did when I came to myself at the bottom of the barrel. I called my daddy. I said, "Daddy, I've blown it. I failed. I'm a mess. Can I come home?"

I still remember that phone call. I'd fallen from second in my class to all F's in one semester. I called my dad, and Dad said, "If you want to come home, I'll come get you." He dropped everything he was doing, picked me up, and took me home. I was still his son, only this time it was by my choice as well as his. He'd given me freedom, let me go and then taken me back. Today we're best friends. He works with me as a key pastor on my staff. We're really close. But it never could have been that way if my parents hadn't loved me enough to give me wings and let me fly.

Now I have children, and it's a lot harder than I thought! Every day I work at those relationships. I pray over them. But there is occasionally a hard day when we don't always understand each other.

God wants our relationships to work, but there's an enemy in the world who is out to rob, destroy and hinder relationships. Satan seeks to destroy interdependent relationships that are healthy or have great potential — those that God has created.

It's not always easy to have good relationships. There's warfare involved. The good news is that we're not alone! God gave us His Holy Spirit to empower us and to help us. And God gave us principles that He says will work if we dare to apply them — to make them habits in our lives.

We've explored the importance of praying for your relationships and maturing into self-acceptance. We discovered the power of treasuring — of building value in other people. God gave us the principle of genuineness, being honest with other people while accepting them as they are. We learned that we can build security in our relationships through commitment. All those things are true, and they have enormous results. All these are habits for winning relationships. But there's more!

Here's a wild one for you. Hang on and don't reject it, until I explain the whole thing. Even God can't make all relationships work! I'm not suggesting that God fails. No, He simply doesn't force Himself into relationships with those who refuse to relate to Him. Not every relationship that God initiates works.

Jesus Christ had one disciple, Judas, whom He loved. For over three years, He tried to make a relationship work. Even at the Last Supper, He tried to redeem Judas. But Judas wouldn't respond. Even Jesus failed with Judas.

What about the relationship Jesus offered to the rich young man? He asked the rich young man to follow Him, but the man went away in sorrow. Jesus loved him but couldn't make the young man love Him in return.

Do you believe God wants everyone to go to heaven? I do. The Bible says God wills that no one should perish but all come to everlasting life. It's just as true, though, that not everyone will make it to heaven. As much as God loves the world, there are some people whom He isn't winning. They resist Him, and He has to let them go.

So, here's the fifth habit of winning relationships: personal freedom. Sometimes we have to realize that relationships don't always work the way we want. Sometimes the ones loved want to go their own way like the prodigal son.

This sixth principle of relationships declares that a relationship is genuine and lasting when both people have the right to choose to stay or leave. A winning relationship has to be by choice; it has to have wings.

## Personal Freedom Means that I Alone
## Can't Make a Relationship Work

We must allow for personal freedom in all our relationships. Your relationships are no better than the choice that people make in that relationship. You alone can't make your relationships work. You can't force a relationship to happen. It's two people by mutual choice who make a relationship work.

You can't make someone like you.
You can't make someone love you.
You can't make someone stay married to you.
You can't make someone stay home.
Relationships have to be by personal choice.

Try all you want, give all you want; do all you can do. If other people don't choose to stay in a relationship with you, you can't make them. You can't rule by force in their heart. They have a choice. Christians don't make slaves out of others in relationships. When you don't give people personal freedom to choose a relationship, they often end up being driven away. When the other person isn't given free choice, you strangle that relationship in spite of everything you want. You can end up harming a relationship more than healing it when you force the relationship or hold on too tightly.

The human tendency is to make people do things. We live in a controlling, manipulating world. We want to control those around us and make them do what we want or what we think best. But the human tendency to control rips relationships apart. It comes from beneath, not from God.

## Holding on Too Tightly Can
## Force Another Person Away

Our family has had both dogs and cats. I've never

"loved" cats. They don't know who's the owner and who's the pet. Besides, I'm allergic to them. One night our cat disappeared. I was blamed for that cat disappearing. Honestly, I didn't touch the cat. He just disappeared. My kids were much younger then. They loved to hold that cat so tightly and cuddle it. They just loved animals.

Well, my son, Matthew Lee, is very aggressive. I don't know where he gets it from! But no matter what he does, he gives it everything he's got. He used to grab this little dog by the throat and say, "Hi, puppy!" The poor dog would be gasping for air! Or he'd grab the cat by the tail and drag it around the house. The poor cat was screaming at the top of its lungs for help.

Matthew couldn't understand why those animals would run away and hide when they saw him. His feelings would be hurt. He'd say, "Daddy, I love the dog and cat. I love to kiss them and hold them tight."

"Matthew," I'd try to explain, "that's why the cat and dog don't respond. You're holding them too tightly. You're bruising them, and you scare them." Finally, the cat had all he could take. He was out of there!

It's the same way in relationships. When you hold on too tightly and don't give other people freedom and choices, you can produce the opposite of what you want. Emotional drift happens when people feel smothered. They feel dominated, and their hearts drift. Outside, you may not see the change right away, but inside, the other person starts drifting further away.

So the relationship may end up in brokenness. You say, "What have I done wrong?" You can love in such a controlling manner that you push the relationship away.

When you neglect the principle of personal choice and freedom in a relationship, whether you mean to or not, you're like a little kid who takes a little precious life and squeezes it, confines it; and that cat or dog — your spouse or friend — begins to panic, to want some air and desperately to get away. We end up pushing those away whom we really are trying to help or to love. We don't mean it. We're doing it for the best. We only want to protect them...or so we say.

The bottom line is that if there isn't a personal choice in a relationship, it can't work. Grandpa once told me: ''It takes two to dance. Or, you can drag a horse to water, but you can't make it drink.'' My grandmother later added, with a twinkle in her eye, ''but you can give them salt and make them thirsty!''

We know that's true. But at times our need to dominate and control completely strangles our relationships. Out of the depths of our needs and our concerns, there comes a point when we begin to violate and abuse that person. We all need space — as much as we need security, commitment, treasuring and valuing. We have to give wings to people for freedom to choose, to grow, to decide the fate of their own lives and their relationships.

Wings are harder to give than roots. I love to protect my kids. And to be very frank, I'm a little concerned what life will be like when my kids are teenagers. It's my solemn hope that Jesus comes back before they have to go out on their own. I mean that sincerely. I don't envy anyone growing up or raising kids in this generation.

I like to tell my son: ''Son, you like good things in life. You like to eat. You like to play. You like to have fun. But if you don't study, Son, if you don't go to a school and get an education, you'll be working for minimum wage somewhere. Then you won't have the kind of things you want." I would love to pour knowledge into his head, sit him down and give him a hunger for knowledge. But I can't.

I'd love to put a cage around my little girl and keep all guys away from her. It makes me cringe to think that some dirty, snotty-nosed kid is going to date my little precious princess. I know he won't be worthy of her. I'd like to say: "Honey, stay home with your daddy all your life. I'll treat you better than any of these guys. You don't need them." But I know I can't. It's not best for either one of us.

I'd love to do things for you, too. I'd love to get you up for prayer in the mornings. I know your day goes better when you pray. I'd love to get you into discipleship and Bible study. I'd like to take your checkbook and show you how powerful God's plan is when you seek God's kingdom first. I'd like you to see how to live in God's Word, read the Bible, pray and fast and experience all those disciplines that produce so much reward in your life. But I can't run your life for you. You have to choose. It only works when you choose to do it yourself from your heart.

You have choices to make. And if you don't give people the right to choose, you damage your relationship. That's exactly what Jesus is telling us in the story of the prodigal son. This parable is more than a sweet story; it holds powerful principles for daily developing winning relationships.

## Seven Principles For Giving Personal Freedom to Others

Releasing others in our relationships is vital for healthy, winning relationships. Here's how to give freedom to others.

**1. Don't be possessive.** You can't own people. You can own things and houses and cars, but you can't own people. Who owns your kids? God does. They're on loan to us, and if you don't recognize that, you begin to squeeze them so hard they may run away.

When you walk down an aisle to get married, that marriage certificate doesn't give you title deed to the soul of the person you married. Try to possess your mate, and you'll begin to strangle that relationship.

**2. Give others the right to privacy.** You know the famous picture of Jesus standing at the door knocking. There's no handle on the outside. The handle is only on the inside. Jesus Christ will never force Himself into your life. He gives you space.

If you love someone enough, you don't have to know every secret and thought he or she has. Everyone needs a private life with God — a place to grow, prosper, think and dream. If you give people space to grow in Christ individually, you can have a better relationship together.

I'm amazed at Mary and Joseph. How wonderful their marriage was! Joseph didn't force Mary to disclose everything God was doing in her life. He could have said to her, "Now, tell me exactly how it happened or what happened or what's going on." Joseph didn't do that, and Mary didn't disclose to Joseph. They gave each other the right to relate to God personally and privately. They were so strong that they could take all the rejection around them and stand firm, because they gave each other the right to develop a private life with God. Your children need space to dream and think and imagine. Give people the right to have some private time.

**3. Encourage other relationships.** What I am trying to tell you here is the word "community." Our society is emotionally becoming warped and damaged. We can see it all around us. Some believe they've discovered the root cause. You know what they believe is causing so much emotional distress in our culture? Cocooning.

Do you know what cocooning is? Cocooning says my wife and my two children are all I need in life. So we go home and close the doors. No one gets in very often, and no one has to go out. We order pizza and rent movies.

Nothing is wrong with family nights. I believe we should have them. But when we isolate ourselves from the Christian community, we magnify our problems. We become out of touch with those who can add to our life.

Have you ever noticed how people tend to stay away from the church when they have problems? As pain increases, we tend to withdraw from others instead of seeking their support and counsel. We begin to pass on our problems from generation to generation.

As hard as you may try, you aren't sufficient alone. God made us to dwell in community. It's in community that we open up, have friends and family, and express ourselves together. In community, you'll learn to give and receive love. God's Spirit works among us, and we grow and nurture and find balance from the body of Jesus Christ. He made you to succeed — not alone nor with just your own intimate family, but as the family of God. We have cocooned to the point we're neglecting and separating ourselves from people with the resources to produce healing in our lives.

I was raised in a wonderful Pentecostal Italian church. By today's standards it wasn't large — about

300 people. It was a wonderful childhood. I was 12 before I realized church members weren't my real family. We called all the adults aunt or uncle. They helped raise me. It was like having a big, caring family.

They'd say, "You're going home with me tonight, Randal. Your mom and dad need a break." I would spend a few days with them, and we had a wonderful time. So, I had family all around. We were community. We learned to love, accept, tolerate, confront and help one another. We learned how to relate. Every Sunday night when I'd go to sleep, there would be 20 people in the house. Everybody was everywhere.

You know what you can learn out of that? You learn tolerance. Uncle George is weird, but you learn to respect Uncle George because he's family. You learn to tolerate and accept and appreciate other people, to value differences and to let others be themselves. All the older women helped the younger women see that child-rearing wasn't so desperate. When Bob was being obnoxious and uptight, all the guys said, "Let's go for a walk. Let's go fishing." They talked to Bob, and they helped him find balance and healing.

Listen to this statement: You don't go to church too much; you go to church too little. I didn't say you need to hear more sermons. You and I need more "Body Life" — more community.

Your husband needs relationships other than you. Your wife needs friends other than you. And your kids need friends. We need other relationships. We all need a little freedom to build healthy, powerful relationships.

**4. Let your relationships grow.** Relationships are never stagnant. They're always changing. Children grow up. Spouses change. Friends go through different passages in life.

I began pastoring my present church at the age of 33. Over the past seven years of ministry, I did some things very well, and I also made some mistakes. But I'm so thankful that my people let me grow as a pastor. When you give others the right to grow and change, you build a lasting bond. And those relationships stay fresh and fulfilling.

**5. Honor the choices others make.** God has given every one of us the right to choose. When someone has made a choice, do your best to live by that choice. When others fail, don't rub it in. Weep with them. Become like the Loving Father in Luke 15, and welcome back the person who has failed. When they succeed, rejoice with them. Learn to honor their choices.

**6. Release them when necessary.** There comes a time when you have done all you can do. You tried your best. You've put as much as you can into the relationship. But it's still not enough. You need to learn to let go.

There may come times when others don't want to be your friends anymore. That's their loss, but you have to let them go. There may come a time when you pray for your mate, and you're separated. You try and you try and you try, but that mate goes through with the divorce.

The other person has the freedom to choose to leave. The Apostle Paul said if your unbelieving mate doesn't want to stay with you because of Christ, let them go. Sometime they may return. I've seen miracles just like the one that opened this chapter. But often, estranged mates won't return. That's the freedom God gives. Learn all you can learn from your failures. Cry and weep, examine and get counseling, if necessary. God will see you through. Learn to let them go, and go on with life. Let them go so that if they come back, you both are different and the relationship is by choice.

**7.   Keep Jesus Christ in the center of your life.** Any time you put another human being besides Jesus Christ in the center of your life, you'll get hurt and you'll hurt other people. We mean well and are sincere. But whenever anyone besides God is in your center, you won't be able to build winning relationships.

We may mean well by making our kids the center of our lives. We may even think we're doing it for God. But children do leave home and may leave town. Then what will happen to our lives without Jesus at the center?

Jesus Christ loves you enough to let you choose where you will spend eternity. That scares me. You have a right to make a choice to serve Him, reject Him, obey Him or rebel against Him. God says, ''I will have no robots.'' You have the freedom to choose or reject an eternal relationship with Jesus Christ. He gives you the freedom you need for a winning relationship with Him or a losing relationship without Him. Choose Jesus Christ now!

Pray and reflect for a moment. Ask yourself these questions:

- Are you holding on too tightly in a relationship with a spouse, friend or child?
- Are you willing to release past, failed relationships?
- Can you give those that you love the freedom to make their own choices in life?
- Will you accept back into your life those who have failed you in the past and need forgiveness and restoration?

If you're holding too tightly, ask God for courage to trust others to God. Give them freedom, and watch the relationship grow. Do it now before it's too late.

# 7

# Habit #6: Accept Others — Even When They're Different

Debbie was three years old when her father kissed her good-bye. She never knew him well, and deep down inside she felt he'd never loved her. Strangely, she blamed herself for his leaving. She thought she just wasn't good enough to make her daddy happy. After the divorce, her mother remarried, but Debbie's fresh expectation of a father's love and acceptance was shattered when her stepfather molested her.

At age 13, she packed up her things and moved in with her neighbors.

Most of her life was packing and moving from one place to another as she ran from relationships. Her brother suffered also. He developed a mental block and began acting like a small boy. Debbie's life was falling apart.

Loneliness and rejection filled her days, and she began to withdraw from everyone. Fear of danger tormented her. Heart pains and headaches were daily occurrences. Problems of lust began to occupy her thought life. And when she began to seek God, all she heard was: "You're not right with God. God will never love you, because you don't measure up." She heard countless sermons on God's love, but in her heart she never thought it was for her.

Like many, Debbie's self-concept depended upon a father's love and acceptance. His rejection began to destroy her self-image. Deep inside, her bruised spirit told her that no one could ever love and accept her. So she became promiscuous, using her body to get the affection she couldn't receive in healthy ways. She was unable to commit herself to others in lasting relationships or believe that someone could really love her.

Debbie felt empty and alone. Into the depths of her rejection came the good news of acceptance. She met Jesus Christ. Through the loving Body of Christ, she and her brother had a marvelous transformation. She is a living testimony to the liberating power of a loving God. At times, Debbie still struggles with self-worth and acceptance. Sometimes she feels the pain of rejection and needs a fresh dose of acceptance.

It's true for all of us, isn't it? We may be healed and forgiven, but we need to be reassured and have a fresh dose of love and acceptance.

One of the deepest bruises that can happen to any of our relationships is the bruise of rejection. Even Christians can reject one another. In Acts 15:36-41, we read of a disagreement between Paul and Barnabas. Barnabas wanted to take Mark with them on a missionary journey, but Paul "did not think it wise to take [Mark]." Acts 15:39 records, "They [Paul and Barnabas] had such a sharp disagreement that they parted company."

Paul rejected Mark. There seemed to be a good reason for this separation, but the logic doesn't soothe the pain of rejection. Years later, Paul and Mark became partners in ministry again. They learned what we all need to learn: All relationships require acceptance to prosper and be healthy. When we're rejected, it destroys our capacity to develop relationships that have true worth. I believe God is speaking to the church about rejection and the need for acceptance.

## The Pain of Rejection

Have you ever felt rejected? I think we all have at crucial times, whether it was when we were cut from the team or when a marriage partner told us we no longer were important to them. Rejection happens to Christians and non-Christians, to families and friends, to parents and children, to bosses and employees, to church leaders and laity.

We all have felt rejection. Rejection hurts, and it can affect almost every aspect of life. The good news is that there is a cure for the pain of rejection. It's the sixth habit of effective, winning relationships. It is the power of genuine acceptance.

We understand acceptance by first facing the bruise of rejection in our lives. When you are rejected by someone — whether it's intentional or not — you get bruised emotionally on the inside. Like physical bruises, some emotional bruises are small and heal easily. Others, however, are so deep they may last a lifetime.

Satan makes it his business to be sure each of us experiences rejection. He sows division in our relationships. His goal is to bruise us deeply enough so we expect and then pass on the pain of rejection to others. The enemy knows that if he can damage us severely enough on the inside, he can keep us from developing winning relationships with God and others.

When rejection is sown, it produces a harvest. The harvest of rejection is inadequacy. Inadequacy is the bruise — the result from the blow of rejection. The person who has been rejected feels inadequate, flawed and unable to live up to the expectations or standards of another.

Verbally or non-verbally, the person doing the rejecting conveys to another person: "You don't have what it takes. You're not good enough to be around me or to relate to me." Sometimes the rejection has little effect upon us. There are also times when rejection goes deep, causing enormous damage that can last a lifetime.

The city we live in has one of the finest Air Force pilot training programs in the world. Every year the young officers come to learn to fly those powerful fighters. For many, it's a lifelong dream.

Not long ago, a pilot told me he was washed out of the training program at Reese Air Force Base. All of his life he had wanted to be pilot, and he didn't make it. He was rejected and he was hurting. He said: "Pastor, you don't understand. My whole life was built around this dream of being a pilot. They said I don't measure up. I don't know what to do with my life."

When you feel rejected and inadequate, it affects your relationships. It becomes increasingly difficult to be genuine, to commit, not to be self-centered when you feel rejected. Rejection is like an avalanche: It starts small, but it can gain great and destructive momentum.

When you feel inadequate, you start looking in all the wrong places to meet your inner needs. That seeking may lead to co-dependence, passiveness, stressful relationships, and, finally, to heartache.

**The Leprosy of Rejection**

The Bible says there's a cure for the damage and

wounds that come from life's rejections. It is the unconditional love and acceptance that God gives us — even when we fail. When you receive acceptance from Christ and acceptance from those who matter in your life, your life is transformed, and your relationships begin to heal and grow.

Acceptance says that you have value — you have a foundation that gives you the ability to reach for the stars! Acceptance frees us to grow up and to dare to build lasting and satisfying relationships.

Rejection is like a form of leprosy. It affects everything you do. It drives you out of healthy relationships. In biblical times, the word for a leper was synonymous with rejection. In Numbers 5:2, we read of how a leper had to be put out of the camp, isolated from contact with others. When anyone approached, the leper would cry out, "Unclean!" so others wouldn't come near.

After a leper had been touched by God and healed, the leper had to go to the priest, who would examine the person and go through a ritual of cleansing. Only then could the leper be accepted by family, friends and society. How lepers must have longed for cleansing and acceptance! How painful their lives of rejection must have been!

In Mark 1:40-45, we read of a leper approaching Jesus and begging to be made clean. He was one of the outcasts, rejected by society and probably his family. But he heard of one who could change that! He knew Jesus had the power to cleanse him. He didn't know if Jesus would accept and cleanse him. But he dared to try. He says to Jesus: "If you want to, You can! If You care enough, will You cleanse me?"

Jesus did something that must have sent a shock wave through the crowd. He not only cared, but He touched an unclean leper. Jesus had compassion, touched and healed him!

That touch of Jesus is the vital part of this encounter! His touch not only released God's power, but it conveyed for all to see that he was accepted. The leper was made whole both internally and physically. He was no longer rejected, but fully accepted. And it changed his life, just as it will yours and mine! No one can feel the accepting touch of God — or even a significant other — and remain the same. It is the power of acceptance to free us from the pain of rejection.

Modern-day lepers, physically afflicted by the disease, are rare in our culture. But spiritual and emotional leprosy abounds through the reality of rejection and feelings of inadequacy. Why is there so much rejection in the world? Why do we sense so much rejection?

Do you realize it's possible to love somebody and still make them feel inadequate? We've all done it, sometimes without even knowing it. You can love your kids or spouse, yet still make them feel inadequate.

We live in a society full of rejection. The slightest little thing can prompt rejection. Sometimes we're trained to believe that the rejection is the result of our failures, our unworthiness or imperfections. We think that if we could just do better, be better, we wouldn't be rejected. We think we have to be perfect to be accepted.

It's not true! Jesus Christ was perfect, yet He experienced rejection. He let no one down. He failed no one. He was without sin. He healed the sick. He raised the dead. He fed the multitudes. He did nothing wrong and was still rejected. No, you don't have to be perfect or a high achiever or pretty to be accepted.

We reject others and they reject us for reasons other than failure and imperfection.

### Why Do People Reject One Another?

There are a few reasons why people reject one another. Some people are just mean and negative. They make it their duty to hurt others. These people intentionally reject others and often find themselves rejected.

Others reject because they don't recognize that God has designed each of us differently, that He wired us up in different ways. If we were raised to believe that differences in methods or views meant that someone was inferior or bad, we live with a warped perspective.

God made us each unique, so that together we might experience a better, fuller life. We are all unique with different personalities. Spiritually, we have differing gifts. (Read 1 Corinthians 12-14.) Mentally, we have unique personalities. And physically, we have particular skills and talents.

A couple whose relationship was in constant conflict came to me for counseling. Their marriage was quickly deteriorating, and they each thought they'd married the wrong person. The truth was that they just didn't understand that God had made them each different, and those differences could be their greatest strength. They failed to understand one of the most basic truths of marriage: that God made men and women differently! They were frustrated because they didn't understand that God made some basic differences between men and women.

Now, I'm not talking about physical differences. There's scientific evidence that suggests women talk more than men. By the time girls reach preschool, virtually all of their words are recognizable, while only 23 percent of boys' words are understandable. Boys are still using many grunts in their responses. Adult women speak on the average of 25,000 words per day. Men speak only half that number. So, when the man has used up his daily quota of words, the woman still has 12,500 words to go!

Men and women emphasize different sides of their brain. Men are usually left-brained; women are usually right-brained. Left brain is the thinking, logical side; the right brain is more creative, feeling and intuitive.

Did you know, though, that women have easier access to both sides of their brain than men do? As a matter of fact, a man's brain in the mother's womb is immersed in a chemical wash that destroys some of the webbing between the two halves of the brain. Men have more difficulty accessing the right side of their brains than women have in using the left side. I wonder if that's why some women accuse men of being slightly brain damaged!

Men look at life differently than women. Men like to conquer. You find that out when you go on a trip with a man. They want to drive from Texas to California in one continuous trip without stopping. Women like the experience of stopping, shopping and taking their time. The journey is more important than the destination.

Men and women see things differently in the relationship. They have different needs. God made our needs different. Men need to be respected. The Bible says this in Ephesians 5:33, ''However, each one of you also must love his wife as he loves himself, and the wife must respect her husband.''

This passage tells it like it is. Men need respect, and women need to be loved and cherished. On a practical level, when a woman feels deprived of love — no matter how much a husband may give to her — she'll experience feelings of rejection. Likewise, the man feels rejected when he senses that his wife doesn't respect him.

Men want to control everything. Women like to change things. The more control a husband attempts in a marriage relationship, the more rejected the wife feels. The more a wife tries to change her husband, the more rejected he feels.

How many marriages are in conflict because we don't realize that God has made us different in what we need from each other! Simply put, winning relationships understand that men and women have many unique differences in the ways they relate to one another. When we learn to accept each other with our God-given uniqueness and differences, we start to build stronger, more satisfying relationships.

When we don't use our knowledge of those unique differences in relationships, Satan can bring confusion and misunderstanding into our marriages. Our prayers can be hindered when we lack knowledge of the other person in a relationship.

## Understand Personality Differences

Gary Smalley and John Trent share some important insights into our personality differences. I want to adapt and share some of my insights with you about the four basic personality types they define in their book, *Home Remedies* — lions, otters, golden retrievers and beavers.

- **Lions** — "Lions are strong, aggressive, take-charge types." We make room for lions. Lions are natural leaders with strong egos. They love conquering problems and facing challenges in life. Lions find themselves highly motivated to solve problems. And they have problems with people not as highly motivated as themselves.

Lions love a challenge and often push themselves and others to the limit to conquer the task. Lions can bring great strength and leadership to winning relationships, to the Body of Christ and to the family. Be careful, however, if more than one lion is around in a group. Conflict may be just around the corner. Lions are great, but too many of them can make life miserable!

My staff and family know I'm a lion type. My wife could tell you some things about how to relate to lions. First of all, get to the bottom line. Don't describe situations with a novel as long as *War and Peace*. Instead, give a *Reader's Digest* version.

Casual talk doesn't make much sense to a lion. Lions may get a lot accomplished, but feelings and relationships may get hurt along the way. My wife has learned that just because I don't want long explanations, I do care about her and the situations she describes. I'm not being hurtful when I ask for the bottom line. I say, "What's the point? Get to the bottom line." Every lion needs someone around him to tell others, "He didn't mean it that way."

The Apostle Paul was a lion. That's what happened in Paul and Barnabas' conflict over John Mark. Paul wanted action — to go on with a missionary journey. The bottom line was more important to him than John Mark's feelings. Barnabas felt differently. So, Paul and Barnabas parted company.

When you understand lions' personality, you know that they may be strong, but they need lots of love and help to make them successful. Lions can learn some things.

- Lions don't like to be questioned. But they need to listen closely to the questions and constructive criticisms of others.

- Lions need to remember that people are more important projects. A lion has a tendency to steam-roll people for the common goal.

- Lions need to be more considerate, kinder and gentler. Lions can't be as hard on people as they are on problems.

- Otters — "Otters: are parties waiting to happen." Otters love to have fun. They look at life as a big celebration. Their favorite verse is, "So if the Son sets you free, you will be free indeed" (John 8:36). Otters make great cheerleaders and motivators. People love to be motivated by otters, because they're always talking and talking and talking. Otters love to help others lighten up and relax.

Characteristically, otters aren't into details. Their time perspective is the future. Lions want everything now. Otters say that we should relax, hold on, be patient, enjoy the moment. I have a great otter on staff named Paul. He dresses for the fun of it. He wears the most outlandish socks and ties just to have fun. He and his perspective are a vital part of our church. He brings joy and a unique perspective of God's grace to our fellowship.

Like lions, though, otters have some things to learn.

- They can procrastinate in solving problems and ignore the problems too long. The otter needs to know deadlines are not guidelines, and a missed deadline might be an opportunity lost forever.

- Otters sometimes need a strong dose of reality. Otters need to know it's more important to please God than to please people.

- **Golden retrievers** — "Golden Retrievers: Loyal and True-Blue." These people are the most deeply committed to others. Barnabas was probably a golden retriever. He stood by John Mark. He believed in him! Golden retrievers are nurturing, supportive and encouraging. They care. They're great healers. They believe in the relationships they have with others and will listen almost endlessly to others. They're often serious.

How do you know if you're a golden retriever? Golden retrievers seek out the hurting people and do everything possible to help. Golden retrievers make great friends. My wife is a golden retriever, and I wouldn't know what to do without her and her perspective.

Golden retrievers, too, have to be careful about certain tendencies.

- They find it hard to say "no" to others, especially when they perceive the person is hurting. They may over-commit to others and finally explode from failing to take care of themselves.

- They may try to please people more than God. Instead of confronting others with the reality of their problems, they may try to fix them or cover up the problems.

- **Beavers** — "Leave it to the beavers." Beavers are the ones who construct and manage the whole world. They're detail oriented. They actually read instructions! Beavers look before they leap and make sure they count the cost of any new undertaking.

They're organized, and may the Lord help you if you change their organization. They order their private world and everyone else around them!

A beaver knows how to set the clock on the video cassette recorder. Beavers line up their shoes in the closet and their socks in the dresser drawer. Beavers get it done. Beavers' perspective is the past. They look back to remember what went right and what went wrong.

A beaver needs to learn:

- How to major in majors, not minors, to avoid getting lost in the details.
- Not to manage relationships so much as to allow spontaneity and sincerity to come through.
- To remember that those who aren't so orderly aren't necessarily bad, but perceive the need for order differently.

I've reviewed these personality differences to remind you that God made us all differently. All of us are important to the Body of Christ. One personality is not more important than another. Since all of us are necessary to construct winning relationships, we need to begin to accept one another as Christ has accepted us.

## Our Relationships Depend Upon Acceptance

Acceptance doesn't mean that we approve of every behavior. But we do accept that others are accepted as God made them, not as we want them to be. You don't have to change to be accepted. That's the key! When we accept others as God's creations and value them without demanding they change, we have the sixth principle that builds healthy, powerful relationships. Certainly, all of us need to grow. But we don't reject a person simply because she's a lion or he's a beaver.

This sixth habit for winning relationships is so essential for healthy relationships. We can accept others because Christ accepted us (Romans 15:7). So parents, children, spouses, friends and church members can accept the personality differences in each other.

Of course, all of us forget this habit at times. We not only try to make others be like us, but we even try to make God be like us! It always ends in disaster when we try to make everyone see life and react as we do.

How do we make acceptance a habit in our relationships? Begin now by making a list of the closest people around you. By each name, identify what kind of personality that person tends to have — lion, otter, golden retriever or beaver.

**Name**                                    **Personality Type**

_____

_____

_____

_____

_____

Now pray for God's love to bring you to accept that person as God created him or her. Pray for God's acceptance to flow through your life in the power of His Holy Spirit.

Do something every day, if possible, that says, "I accept you as you are." Decide to accept others as God accepts you! Learn to tap the resources and perspective that others have. God has brought them to your life to make your life better.

Even if it's frustrating for a time, remember that God's greatest power comes to our lives when we all share love and acceptance with one another.

Pray this prayer with me:

*"Heavenly Father, I thank You for this new understanding of acceptance. I accept myself, and now I accept others who are different from me because You made them for a special purpose. Make me a healing instrument to release others from their bruises of inadequacy. Let the love and character of Christ live through me this day. Amen!"*

# 8

# Habit #7: Forgive!

The final habit of winning relationships is the most important and necessary of all. It is forgiveness. You simply can't have a truly winning relationship without receiving and giving forgiveness. Forgiveness must be understood and applied to every relationship, because everyone of us is a sinner.

Sin is not a popular concept in our day. But it's one that must be taken seriously. The Bible tells us that every one of us sins. That means we all fail. When you fail, you need to experience forgiveness. And when you fail others, you must learn to forgive them. Without forgiveness, no relationship can survive. Relationships don't fail just because there's sin, but because there's too often a lack of forgiveness.

Throughout this book, we've referred to Jesus' parable of the prodigal son a number of times. This parable is primarily about forgiveness on two levels. First, there's the forgiveness of the wayward son who returns to his forgiving father. But there's a second level in this story, one that's often overlooked: The unforgiving, bitter brother. What a contrast between sons and between father and oldest son!

Remember the story in Luke 15:11-32? It's fascinating to me, because the older son is out working hard for the father. He comes in, sees this party and asks his servant what it all means. The older brother is told that his younger brother has returned, and Dad has killed the best calf in honor of his brother's homecoming. Not only that, the father has put an expensive robe and ring on the younger brother — all for one who had failed miserably and hurt the family.

Now, everyone is having a great time except the older brother. You know how the younger son felt? He was feeling great! He was forgiven. When the father demonstrated forgiveness, it lifted their relationship to an all-time high! The younger son knew nothing could take him away again. That's the power and joy of forgiveness.

But the older brother is filled with resentment. He doesn't go in to enjoy the party. The father goes out to his older son and asks him to join the celebration. The brother refuses, and out of his gut comes years of slop-bucket resentment. Do you know what a slop bucket is? It's the pail that all the garbage was thrown into and used to feed the hogs on the farm. It really smelled when left too long in the house!

You can just hear the older brother. He pulls out his list that he's been waiting for years to dump on Dad. He says something like this: "See, all these years I've been faithful to you, and you never gave me a party. You've always made me work hard, and I never crossed you. I've always been on your side."

A child may say, "Yes, sir!" and even obey but still harbor resentment. The younger son had revealed his sinful attitude to his father at the beginning of the parable. But the older son had apparently hidden his resentment for years — until it began to destroy his relationship with his own father. The father responds with love, encouraging the older son not to have the same destructive attitude that the prodigal son had suffered.

God doesn't tell us how this story ends. Did the older brother go in or did he stay out? Did he come and join the party or did he run away? We aren't told, because I believe that each of us has to write our own ending to the story with our lives and our relationships. This powerful story does tell us some important things about how to live in the power of forgiveness.

### The Power of Forgiveness

The Bible tells us that forgiveness has enormous power. Forgiveness has the power to set free people's spirits that are bound up and destroyed through sin, and Satan's dominion, possession and ownership. Forgiveness has the power to take broken, hurting relationships and restore them to a fresh love.

Do you believe that? Do you remember a time when your life was bound by guilt and sin, and God set you free? Do you know how it feels when you hear God say to you, "You're a sinner, but I forgive you and restore you to full position as a child of God"? It's a miracle — one of the greatest miracles in the world. There is no psychologist, no medicine, no tranquilizer, no aspirin, no vacation that can do what forgiveness can do for you and then through you to others.

Forgiveness can heal your body. To put it another way, unforgiveness can make you sick, give you ulcers, arthritis and migraine headaches. I've read of medical doctors talking about emotions like resentment and unforgiveness triggering cancer in us. I've seen physically sick people who were wrapped up in unforgiveness. When they came to Jesus Christ and asked for forgiveness, God's Holy Spirit healed them physically and spiritually. James 5:16 says, "Confess your sins to each other and pray for each other so that you may be healed.''

When you see resentment and unforgiveness for what they are, it's easier to let them go. Resentment is...

- a storehouse in our spirit where the results of old, unconfessed sins keep us in bondage.

- a slop bucket and garbage pail that stinks up our relationships — no matter how much we try to freshen up our behavior with excuses and denials.

- a nice word we try to use to justify hate.

- an unforgiving spirit that looks for ways to get even, to punish, or to hold onto pain and hurt.

There are no winners when forgiveness is withheld in a relationship. May I also suggest to you that forgiveness is greatly misunderstood. While we may think we know what forgiveness is, let me tell you first what it is not!

**Forgiveness Is Not...**

- condoning the destructive or sinful action of another person.

- taking blame upon ourselves for another's guilt.

- earned or deserved because the other person pacified us.

- making other people pay for their guilt.

- trying to teach the other person something.

- feeling sympathy or pity.

- becoming a doormat or being weak.

- making light of the sin.

**Forgiveness Is...**

Having said all of that, here's what forgiveness is:

- to erase.
- to cut off the debt.
- to release an account that is due.
- to give up the right to hold on to the hurt any longer.
- to wipe the slate clean.
- to offer reconciliation, regardless of how the other person responds!

Forgiveness is the ultimate requirement of lasting relationships, because we know that we all fail. Forgiveness doesn't just forgive once, but as often as is necessary. One of the most radical portions of scripture is Matthew 18:21-22, where Peter asks, "Lord, how many times shall I forgive my brother when he sins against me? Up to seven times?"

Jesus answered, "I tell you, not seven times, but seventy-seven times." In other words, Jesus insists that our forgiveness must be limitless. Forgiveness must be a lifestyle, a commitment to never allow the sun to go down on your anger lest it turns into resentment (Ephesians 4:26).

Anger is not sin. God gets angry 127 times in the Bible. The Bible says God was angry, and God can't sin. There's a place for righteous anger. For example, righteous anger with abortion can motivate us to work for change in our society. We're building a ministry for unwed mothers that provides complete care and counseling for birth, not abortion.

Righteous anger motivates you to do something. Sinful anger rooted in bitterness paralyzes, blinds and destroys you. Resentment wants to get even; forgive-

ness wants to restore. Unforgiveness destroys relationships; forgiveness heals relationships and keeps them
growing.

Forgiveness is the only thing in the Bible you have
to give to keep. Jesus says, "For if you forgive men
when they sin against you, your heavenly Father will
also forgive you. But if you do not forgive men their
sins, your Father will not forgive your sins" (Matthew
6:14-15).

Do you believe God is serious about that? Do you
understand how hard that is? What Jesus is saying is
that we can't afford the price of unforgiveness. We
can't afford resentment. We can't afford to get even
or to harbor revenge. These are Satan's tools of
destruction.

Bruce Thielemann tells a story of Simon
Wiesenthal, a prisoner in a Polish concentration camp
in World War II. He only wanted to survive. The Nazis
assigned him to a hospital for German soldiers coming
back from the Russian front. He tells of how a nurse
came, grabbed his arm and said, "Come with me."
She took him to the bed of an SS trouper, a 22-year-
old man named Franze. The dying SS trouper was
bleeding profusely. Franze took Sam's hand and said,
"I have to talk to a Jew." He began to pour out this
tragic story to Simon.

"We were on the Russian front. Our commander
made us pour 20 gallon tanks of gasoline all over this
house. Then he made us march 200 Jews inside this
house so close together that they could not move. Then
we were ordered to throw grenades into the windows
and watch as they exploded and burned.

"Then we were ordered to shoot anyone who
jumped out of the windows. We threw the grenades,
and in the second story window, I saw a father holding

a little baby boy in his arms. As the flames were on his back, he covered his son's eyes with his free hand. Then he jumped out the window. A second later, his wife jumped to him.

"Oh, God, we shot and killed them. I can never get it out of my mind. I know what I have done is terrible, but if you can only forgive me, then I can die in peace."

Here is a German Nazi on his deathbed asking a Jewish prisoner in a concentration camp to forgive him. The Nazis were starving Simon to death. He was being abused. He had learned that these German soldiers had just done a horrible deed against his people.

Simon did what most of us would be tempted to do. He said nothing. He pulled his hand free from the German's grasp and just walked away. You might think that Simon felt free and vindicated. No, just the opposite. For the rest of his life, he was tormented with the thought of his unforgiveness. Forgiveness may be hard and even expensive, but it is much cheaper and much easier than unforgiveness.

## The Ultimate Habit For Winning Relationships Is Forgiveness

For every relationship to thrive and grow, it must give and receive forgiveness. The ultimate gift in a winning relationship that we can give one another is forgiveness. You need forgiveness. You need it from God, and you need it from those whom you have failed. We may need it from our children, our wives, our husbands, our parents, our employees, our boss, our friends, our neighbors. We may need it from our students or from our teachers, but we all need it! It is not easy to forgive or receive forgiveness! But there's no power quite like it!

Forgiveness has the power to restore and protect the most precious possession in the world: relationships! When you know you'll be forgiven when you fail, you're free to build a relationship nothing can destroy. When those around us know they can count on genuine forgiveness, they're set free to soar in life, to reach and to dare to fail!

Forgiveness frees us from the fear of failure. We're all sinners, and sin destroys. It destroys lives, nations, families, marriages. The solution to sin is God's forgiveness working through each of us. The more you give it, the greater its power in our lives!

### How Do You Give the Gift of Forgiveness?

Here are a few basic steps to take.

• Recognize your own need for forgiveness. We constantly need God's forgiveness. Pride hinders us from asking for it, and pride blocks our forgiveness of others. Forgiving others begins with humbly admitting our need to be forgiven. I find it much easier to forgive when I'm aware of my own need for forgiveness.

• Keep your eyes on Christ. We need His power in our lives to forgive. At times we can't find the strength to forgive. We need help. When we see God's great love and His mercy toward us — even at our worst — it changes our perspective. Forgiveness is always easier when your eyes are on Christ.

• **Be committed to forgiveness before the hurt ever happens.** Forgiveness is hard to give in the midst of pain and hurt. Don't wait until you've been hurt to decide whether or not you're a forgiving person. Commitment is a decision to obey God before obedience is required. Decide in advance that your attitude will be: ''There's nothing you can do to make me not forgive you! There may have to be correction involved, but I'll never withhold forgiveness from you with God's help.''

• **Forgive yourself when God forgives you.** Read 1 John 3:20-22. What the Bible is telling you and me is that God can forgive us anything we confess (1 John 1:9). Still, there are times when God forgives us but we can't let go of our guilt and sin. We can't forgive ourselves. Let go of the guilt. Forgive yourself when God forgives you. When you dare to forgive yourself, you can forgive others.

• **Forgive daily.** Don't store up unforgiveness. Refuse to put off forgiving someone who has wronged or hurt you. Forgive now.

• **Allow time for healing.** Forgiveness isn't an instant solution. Forgiveness may be given in a moment, but healing takes time. Stop being so hard on yourself or others. Forgiveness doesn't mean instant healing. Saying or receiving ''I forgive you'' doesn't right every wrong instantly. Healing takes time.

## The Angel of Forgiveness

Here is an ancient story. In a little village, there lived a thin baker named Fouke. His wife, Hilda, was short and round. Hilda respected her righteous husband and loved him, but her heart ached for more than righteousness.

One morning Fouke came home and found a stranger in his bed lying with his wife. Hilda's adultery soon became the talk of the town. Everyone assumed Fouke would cast Hilda out of his house, so righteous was he. But he surprised everyone by keeping Hilda as his wife, saying he forgave her as the Good Book said he should.

However, in his heart, Fouke could not forgive Hilda for bringing shame to his name. Whenever he thought about her, his feelings toward her were angry and harsh. He despised and resented her, for she had hurt him and his reputation. He only pretended to forgive Hilda so that he could punish her with his self-righteousness.

Fouke's fakery didn't sit well in heaven. Each time Fouke felt his secret hate toward Hilda, an angel would come to him and drop a small pebble, hardly the size of a shirt button, into his heart. Each time a pebble dropped, Fouke would feel a stab of pain — like the pain he felt the moment he discovered Hilda's sin. He resented her more and more. His hate brought him pain, and his pain multiplied his hate.

The pebbles piled up, and Fouke's heart grew very heavy — so heavy that the top half of his body bent forward. He was so bent over that he had to strain his neck upward to see straight ahead. Fouke began to wish he were dead.

The angel who dropped the pebbles into Fouke's heart came to him one night and told him how he could be healed. Fouke would need the miracle of spiritual eyes. Through spiritual eyes, he'd be able to see his Hilda not as a wife who betrayed him but as a weak woman who needed him. Only a new way of looking at things through spiritual eyes could heal the hurt flowing from the wounds of Fouke's past.

At first, Fouke protested. "Nothing can change the past. Hilda is guilty. That's a fact not even an angel can change."

"Yes, poor hurting man, you're right," the angel replied. "You can't change the past. You can only heal the hurt that comes to you from the past. That healing only comes through the vision of new eyes."

"How can I get new eyes?" Fouke asked.

"Only ask — desiring as you ask — and they'll be given you. Each time you see Hilda through your new eyes, one pebble will be lifted from your aching heart," the angel instructed.

Fouke couldn't ask at once, for he had grown to love his hatred. But the pain of his heart finally drove him to want and to ask for the eyes the angel had promised. So he asked, and the angel gave. Soon Hilda began to change in front of Fouke's eyes. He began to see her as a needy woman who loved him — not a wicked woman who had betrayed him.

The angel did as he had promised and lifted the pebbles one at a time. It took a long time for all of them to be taken away.

Gradually, Fouke felt his heart grow lighter. He began to walk straight again. Somehow, his face grew less sharp than before. He invited Hilda back into his heart again. Together, they began a renewed relationship in joy.

Are you weighted down with the burden of resentment and unforgiveness? Right now, list the people you need to forgive. How will you forgive them? By letter? By phone? Face to face?

What about forgiveness for you? Are you ready to ask God in Jesus Christ to forgive you of past guilt and failure? Are you ready to forgive yourself?

Pray with me:

*"Heavenly Father, forgive me of my resentment and of holding onto my hurt. Empower me to forgive others daily. As I forgive others, lift the heavy burden of self-righteousness from me. I claim the cross of Christ now for power to forgive and be forgiven. Amen."*

# POSTSCRIPT

All of us want winning relationships. These seven basic habits — built on God's Word and learned through the teaching of the Holy Spirit — can transform our relationships...

from hopeless to hopeful,
from destructive to constructive,
from powerless to powerful,
from hurting to helping
and from losing to winning.

So, stop just sitting there reading a book! Get up and get started in living these seven habits. They really work.

- Love and accept yourself.
- Commit to others.
- Forgive yourself and others...Now!
- Accept people and their personalities as they are.
- Deposit treasure into the lives of others.
- Release past guilt and failure.
- Be genuine.

These aren't just more good ideas, but principles guaranteed by God! They work. They're not easy. They're not cheap. Like everything worthwhile, godly habits have a price tag. But the good news is that they really work. They release into our lives that which we all crave — healthy, satisfying, winning relationships.

They only work when we apply them. They won't help us by simply reading them. We have to apply them — sow them into the lives of others to reap a wonderful harvest.

There's a story of a city reporter who went to do a story on a successful country farmer. Both the reporter and the farmer were Christians. The reporter asked the farmer, "Aren't you grateful for the blessings of God upon your farm? Why, look at this wonderful farm, the bountiful crops without weeds, the beautiful barn and healthy livestock. The pretty house with fresh paint.''

After the reporter had finished, the farmer quietly replied, "Yes, I'm very grateful for God's blessings. He is my Senior Partner. Without His help, I'd have nothing. But you should have seen it when God had it all by Himself!''

Now, that story can offend us at first reading. But there's a real truth for us. God wants to be our partner, but we have to work His plan for the crop to grow.

I challenge you today to begin. You may have a long way to go, but it's not impossible. You just have to take it one step at a time. If you feel as if you can't, ask God for help.

Feel like it's impossible? Claim for yourself, "With God, all things are possible!'' Remember, relationships are God's idea. With Him, you can have winning relationships! I'm praying for you that all your relationships will be winning in Jesus Christ!

# DISCOVER HOW TO BUILD WINNING RELATIONSHIPS IN TODAY'S CHANGING WORLD

Now you can build and strengthen
your relationships in all of life —
at work, play, or school, at home and in your church.

Discover your own personality traits and relational skills. Plus, learn the important, winning habits for relationships, such as:

- Releasing Your Past Guilt and Failures

- Being Genuine

- Depositing Treasure into Others

- Committing to Others

- Forgiving Self and Others

- Uncovering the Power of Acceptance

- Loving Yourself

*Seven Habits of Winning Relationships* is your personal handbook to guide you into successful and more fulfilling relationships.

**RANDAL ROSS** pastors the 7,000+ Trinity Church in Lubbock, Texas. He is a noted speaker and conference leader for national and international Christian events. He hosts a daily radio ministry that is heard throughout West Texas and New Mexico.